What If You Got Involved?

Taking a Stand Against Social Injustice

What If You Got Involved?

Taking a Stand Against Social Injustice

Graham Gordon

PATERNOSTER PRESS

First published in 2003 by Paternoster Press

09 08 07 06 05 04 03   7 6 5 4 3 2 1

Paternoster Press is an imprint of Authentic Media,
P.O. Box 300, Carlisle, Cumbria, CA3 0QS, UK
and
P.O. Box 1047, Waynesboro, GA 30830-2047, USA

Website: www.paternoster-publishing.com

British Library Cataloguing in Publication Data
A catalogue record for this book is available from the British Library

ISBN 1-84227-243-8

Cover Design by FourNineZero
Typeset by WestKey Ltd, Falmouth, Cornwall
Printed in Great Britain by Cox & Wyman, Reading, Berkshire

To mum and dad

Contents

Foreword

The last few decades have seen an amazing awakening of the social conscience among evangelical Christians all over the world. To be sure, there are still, especially among the well-to-do, those who would like to convince us that the mission of the church should be restricted to 'saving souls' and 'planting churches'. Rooted in a body–soul dualism which reflects Greek philosophy rather than biblical teaching, that understanding of the Christian mission is, however, definitely giving way to a view that is more biblical and, at the same time, more relevant to the contemporary world. That is the view that this book represents.

One of the great merits of this book is that it reflects what the author has learned not only from books but also from actual immersion in situations where the transforming power of the gospel is at work; and not only from Westerners who theorise on development work, but also from practitioners in the Two-Thirds World.

Another value of this book is that it shows the relevance of an interdisciplinary approach to theology – an approach that is synthesized in the title, 'Biblical Foundations for Involvement in Issues of Social Injustice'. Throughout the history of the church, especially in the West, much has been done to ascertain 'biblical convictions' – the concern has been with *orthodoxy*. Unfortunately, not enough has been done with regard to one of the main purposes of Bible study, namely, involvement in the struggle for justice – the question of *orthopraxis*. Graham Gordon has broken down the traditional dichotomy between orthodoxy and orthopraxis. As a result, he has succeeded in making a beautiful symbiosis of the two aspects of God's commandment in which Jesus Christ synthesised the law and the prophets: love to God and love to one's neighbour. In biblical terms, 'anyone who does not love his brother, whom he has seen, cannot love God, whom he has not seen' (1 Jn. 4:20).

In his search for the biblical foundation for Christian social involvement the author could not have done any better than he has done in selecting one of the most comprehensive biblical concepts – the kingdom of God. As many Bible scholars have recognised, that was certainly the centre of Jesus' ministry and message. Properly understood, it provides a solid basis for a view of the mission of the church which transcends not only the individualism but also the ecclesiocentrism that have characterised much of Western missiology. As Gordon demonstrates, a kingdom approach to mission makes it quite clear that our concern for justice is far more than an expression of good will – it is rooted in God's character marked by justice, which involves his special concern for the poor, the marginalised, the weak and oppressed.

Good theology is not only biblical, it is also practical, and Gordon has done well in showing that. One way in which he does it is by giving examples of holistic or integral mission from around the world. The work of reconciliation and healing in Rwanda, the provision of an alternative to prostitution in the Philippines, the liberation of prisoners in Peru, the socio-political involvement in Kenya, and the overcoming of disabilities in Cambodia which he describes are powerful illustrations of kingdom mission in different fields of human need and in different countries. Whoever reads about them can hardly claim that the author has not made clear what he is talking about when he refers to 'a Christian response to social injustice'.

Gordon's concern to combine theory and practice comes through with full force in his discussion on values and vision for change. Since change for the sake of change can hardly be commended from a Christian perspective, the criteria that he suggests for discerning the priorities for social involvement are most essential. After all, as he states, 'We are called not just to work for change, but to do so in a way that will glorify God, maintaining our values and integrity of character.'

Already in the Introduction we are told that this book is 'aimed at both development practitioners in the field who are struggling with how to address some of the underlying injustices they are faced with, and at Christians in the West who want to add their voice to those who are speaking out to make a difference'. Gordon is well aware that different circumstances demand different approaches on the part of Christians involved in the struggle for justice. Practitioners who read this book will find a great deal of practical suggestions and much encouragement for their work. Christians in the West, on the other hand, will not only be challenged *to do something* about injustice but will also find guidelines to move from a passive attitude to the role of campaigners who make a difference to the situation of the poor for the sake of the kingdom of God.

C. René Padilla
International President
Tearfund – UK & Ireland

Preface

This is a joint book between Tearfund and the Micah Network. It is based on a previous discussion paper, *The Mission of the Church and the Role of Advocacy*, jointly written with Bryan Evans. It also draws heavily on Tearfund's *Advocacy Toolkit*.

Tearfund[1] is an evangelical Christian relief and development agency working through local partners to bring help and hope to communities in need, with a vision to see lives and communities transformed. Tearfund supports programmes in around seventy countries in Africa, Asia, Latin America and Europe and this work includes:

- Helping communities to achieve lasting change – in health-care, education and other areas of basic human need.
- Preparing for and responding to disasters.
- Speaking out with, and on behalf of, those who are poor.
- Helping people to earn a living in a sustainable way.

The Micah Network[2] brings together more than 250 evangelical Christian organisations providing relief, development and justice ministries throughout the world. The majority are community development agencies in the Two-Thirds World. The Network has three objectives:

- Strengthening the capacity of participating agencies to make a biblically shaped response to the needs of the poor and oppressed.

- Speaking strongly and effectively regarding the nature of the mission of the church to proclaim and demonstrate the love of Christ to a world in need.
- Prophetically calling upon and influencing the leaders and decision makers of societies to 'maintain the rights of the poor and oppressed and rescue the weak and needy'.

The World Evangelical Alliance and the Micah Network are creating a global evangelical campaign, the Micah Challenge, to mobilise Christians against poverty. The campaign's goals look both inwards, to a deepening of evangelical commitment to the poor, and outwards, to influence leaders to implement policy changes that could dramatically and sustainably reduce poverty. It will bring together millions of evangelical Christians to contribute a prophetic and powerful voice for the poor.

The campaign will target policy change at all levels needed to achieve the Millennium Development Goals, a universally agreed road map towards the halving of key poverty indicators by 2015.

Acknowledgements

I am grateful to Tearfund for giving me leave from my normal work to write this book. I am especially grateful to Andy Atkins and Dewi Hughes for their constant support and direction and extensive comments on various drafts.

Thanks also to Lucy Atherton, Melissa Bodenhamer, Steve Bradbury, Siobhan Calthrop, Bryan Evans, David Evans, Arthur Karobia, Esther Palmer and Alfonso Wieland, who have commented at various stages in the book's development. Thanks also to Tony Graham who has edited the manuscript.

And to all those who helped me in gathering the material for the case studies: John Wesley Kabango, Michel Kayitaba, Froduald Munyankiko and Antoine Rutayisire in Rwanda; Zeny Ablang, Jenny Galvez, Jean Barcena, Melba Maggay and Jonathan Nambu in the Philippines; Omweri Angima, Peter Gitau, Arthur Karobia, James Mageria, Virginia Maina, Mutava Musyimi, Oliver Simuyu, Kamotho Waiganjo and Paul Wangai in Kenya; Glen Miles and Sam Ouern in Cambodia; Nick Buxton, Angela Ditchfield, Audrey Miller, Ben Niblett and Stephen Rand for Jubilee 2000; and Christian Allsworth, Dan Chapman and Mike Hooper for the UK case studies.

Finally, thanks to Luke and Shona Taylor, who kindly allowed me to set up an office in their house to write the book.

Graham Gordon
April 2003

Introduction

When researching for this book, I visited a community in the south of Cambodia. After thirty minutes on the back of a motorbike driving down dusty roads, we arrived at three houses clustered together. They were surrounded by paddy fields with a few coconut trees nearby, at lest ten minutes walk from their nearest neighbours. The houses, built on short stilts, with strips of reeds for the walls and roof, consisted of a single room where the whole family ate, slept and huddled together under a tarpaulin if the weather was bad. The roof wasn't strong enough to keep the rain out.

At the time of our visit, one family was re-weaving their walls so all of their possessions were laid bare for everyone to see. Visible were a few blankets, a tarpaulin, some pots and pans and a handful of clothes. To get enough water to cook and wash they have to walk long distances and carry the water back. They also need to walk miles to the nearest health clinic and even then they may not be able to afford the most basic medicines. Even though school is free, the children do not attend because they cannot afford the schoolbooks and the families need them to help in the fields.

I was told that the rice they grow lasts for eight months, resulting in a four-month hunger gap each year. They sometimes manage to supplement their rice with vegetables or meat. During the hunger gap the men try and find work in other people's fields, as well as their own, in order to earn money to buy enough food to survive.

The main reason for going to visit these houses was because one family had a child with disabilities. Born with polio, he was abandoned by his parents when he was seven months old. He now lives with his grandmother and they struggle together to survive. Thirty community members had gathered around for our visit, including a group of small children and some old men. Sam, who works for a local development organisation, had brought me there. He asked in front of everyone, 'so, what do you think of what you see?' I thought many things, none of which I felt able to say in front of them.

Obviously, I only had a brief insight into their lives. My first reaction was of compassion, confronted by a situation of such stark poverty. However, I also admired their resilience and the ways that the members of the community supported each other. We were only visiting this family because one community member had alerted Sam to the fact that there was a disabled child living there who was ostracised and could not go to school.

I then thought 'why do people have to live like this?' These families are typical of millions of others around the world who, usually through accident of birth or factors beyond their control, are condemned to lives of poverty and injustice. It simply isn't fair. Surely this isn't the type of world that God wants? Surely this isn't how it is meant to be?

This book was written to show that this is indeed not the kind of world that God has in mind. He cares passionately about the poverty of the Cambodian families I met. He cares about injustice and his kingdom is good news to the poor. It is good news for them because it means a restored relationship with God through faith in Jesus and restored relationships with others. It is also good news because they will experience something of the peace, justice and material blessing that is a foretaste of things to come.

As Christians we are privileged to be used by God to bring about his kingdom, to work with him to transform the world into the one that he wants. One of the most striking metaphors for this is the need to be 'salt and light' in the world – to show the truth and to prevent decay. We are motivated by compassion, and this compassion, inspired by God, touches the whole of life. It should make us concerned about the injustice that blights the life of the poor. We should not just be concerned about their eternal salvation.

This book is aimed at Christians who want to make a difference in the world through tackling some of the injustices they see around them. It is for those who want to become more involved in the issues that affect their local community. It is also for those in the west who want to engage with institutions, such as governments and businesses, in their own countries that contribute to injustice, poverty and oppression in poorer countries. Finally, it is for those who are already professional development practitioners who are struggling with how to address some of the underlying injustices they face on a daily basis.

Short-term relief and welfare provision and long-term development projects are essential to help alleviate some of this suffering, to develop a better standard of living and transform communities. However, suffering is often due to systems and structures that are biased against the poor, and policies and laws that are unjust and oppressive. There is therefore a need to tackle the deeper causes of this suffering and become involved in issues of social justice.

One of the answers to 'why do people have to live like this?' is because the church has been absent from so many places and Christians have been silent in too many situations of injustice. In fact, the church has often been complicit and allowed unjust structures and situations to continue. The church and individual Christians need to get more involved.

The title of the book, *What If You Got Involved?*, is derived from the final speech given by Martin Luther King Jr on the night before he was assassinated. He was comparing the reaction of the priest and the Levite to that of the Good Samaritan on the road to Jericho:

> And so the first question that the priest asked, the first question the Levite asked was: 'if I stop to help this man, what will happen to me?' But then the Good Samaritan came by, and he reversed the question: 'if I do not stop to help this man, what will happen to him?'[1]

So the challenge today is to consider what our own community and the wider world will be like if we do not get involved. But the challenge is wider. It is for each Christian to dream about what the world could be like if we did get involved, and to work to make those dreams a reality. If this book helps you to do so, it will have achieved its purpose.

What if you got involved? What if we all got involved?

Negative Responses to Social Involvement

Many Christians are still extremely wary of any talk of involvement in issues of social justice, and remain to be convinced of its biblical basis or its practical usefulness. Views are likely to be influenced by a number of factors and it is good to be aware of these from the outset, so that we know we are not approaching this issue from a neutral position, but come with existing theological views, personal experiences, political contexts and church backgrounds.

Some see any involvement as compromising when it requires engagement in the 'political' sphere. They see politics as corrupt and corrupting. It is not something that Christians who want to remain pure should be involved in.

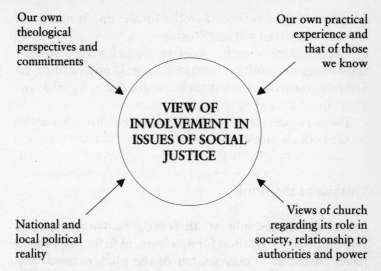

Our own theological perspectives and commitments

Our own practical experience and that of those we know

VIEW OF INVOLVEMENT IN ISSUES OF SOCIAL JUSTICE

National and local political reality

Views of church regarding its role in society, relationship to authorities and power

Passages like Romans 13 (obedience to the government) are used by others to justify lack of action or lack of criticism of those in power.

Another common approach is to split the world into two, the sacred and the secular. Faith and religion are seen as part of the spiritual world and as personal issues. The church can concern itself with them. Reason and science are seen as part of the material world and deemed as public issues. The state can concern itself with them. Values are therefore seen as personal with little relation to the public realm. These two worlds have little overlap. The church should leave matters of social justice to the state. The task of the church is to focus exclusively on preaching the gospel for individual salvation. This means it should opt out of public life altogether.

There is also the belief that this world is in decay and is heading for total destruction, so there is little point working to make it better. Redemption is limited to the personal sphere. Supporters of this view will often argue that the kingdom of God is limited to the future, and is not being worked out in our current world.

Finally, many churches exist in countries with authoritarian regimes and are afraid to speak out or may be severely restricted in what they can do, due to limited religious freedom and existing persecution.

These negative attitudes are addressed throughout the book, both theologically and practically.

Outline of the Book

The book has been split into three sections. The first section is the biblical foundation for involvement in issues of social justice. Chapter 1 outlines ten of the main reasons why Christians do not get involved, and offers some initial responses, which are then developed later on in the book. Chapter 2 sets the context for the mission of the church by looking at the story of God establishing his kingdom. People enter the kingdom by believing in Jesus and the communities these disciples form are the visible sign of the kingdom on earth. God chooses to use them in many ways, including working for social justice, holding those in power to account, as well as caring for those in need, evangelism, prayer and worship. Chapter 3 considers social justice and good news to the poor as central themes of the kingdom. It also looks at the role of the state and the need for God's people to hold authorities to account.

Chapter 4 deals with understanding and grappling with the powers, recognising that the kingdom of the world has set itself up in opposition to the kingdom of God. We are part of this battle and need to put on the full armour of God in order to both protect ourselves and be effective. Chapter 5 considers Jesus' approach to power and politics, showing that he was by very nature a political person, but in a different way to others of his day. Chapter 6 looks at the history of Christian political involvement using both positive and negative experiences to draw out some lessons we can learn for today.

The second section (chapters 7–12) covers experiences from around the world. It highlights the wide range of ways that Christians are tackling issues of social injustice. Experiences cover reconciliation and healing between Hutus and Tutsis after the genocide in Rwanda; working with prostitutes in the Philippines to provide an alternative lifestyle and to change the law that victimises them; defending unjustly condemned prisoners in Peru; holding politicians to account and monitoring elections to reduce violence in Kenya; educating communities and lobbying the government to integrate children with disabilities in Cambodia; and campaigning for debt relief for the world's poorest countries though Jubilee 2000. The aim of this section is to tell the stories of those who are intimately involved in the issues, looking at the successes and the struggles they have faced.

The third section details practical ways to get involved. Chapter 13 is aimed mainly at campaigners in the UK who want to get involved in international issues. Chapter 14 offers suggestions on how to get more involved in your local community, with an outline of how to plan for effective change. Chapters 15 and 16 take some of the issues deeper and are slightly more technical. Chapter 15 discusses Christian distinctiveness by looking at what vision should drive us, what values should be at the centre of our work and how to engage in policymaking. Chapter 16 briefly treats two issues that often cause problems for Christians, namely civil disobedience and human rights.

This book has been written to help people to understand both the biblical and practical imperative to get involved in issues of social justice. There are questions at the end of each chapter. These have been written to help reflection and application. It is a good idea to take some time, even ten minutes, to look over the questions and think more deeply about what you have read. The questions can be answered individually or in a group. If you are reading it yourself, it may be a good idea to find someone with whom you can share your thoughts and discuss the ideas that develop.

On a final note, sometimes the extent of suffering in the world can be overwhelming. We turn off the TV and hope it goes away. We can become apathetic and think that nothing we can do will make any difference. However, when we shift our focus from ourselves to a God who is sovereign and the creator and sustainer of the universe, our perspective will change. Two of Jesus' sayings can bring us comfort and hope here. The first is when he was being arrested and says 'do you think I cannot call on my Father, and he will at once put at my disposal more than twelve legions of angels?' (Mt. 26:53). Jesus was in control, but voluntarily gave up his power. He can do anything he chooses and will do all that is necessary to bring about his kingdom, although its fullness will not be established until he returns. The second is when the disciples are trying to drive out a demon and Jesus says 'I tell you the truth, if you have faith as small as a mustard seed, you can say to this mountain, "Move from here to there" and it will move. Nothing will be impossible for you' (Mt. 17:20). The point is not how much faith you have but in whom you put that faith.

The smallest grain of faith in an all-powerful God can move mountains. It can also tackle the worst cases of in-justice, suffering and oppression. Whether we believe this or not will determine how we live our Christian lives.

We have to make sure our faith is in the right place.

Is your God big enough?

Section 1

Biblical Foundations for Involvement

1

Ten Reasons Not to Get Involved

Introduction

I have heard numerous arguments against involvement in issues of social justice. They are usually a mixture of theological and practical reasons, and they all need to be taken seriously. Some reasons stem from a misunderstanding or incomplete understanding of what the Bible says about God's plan for the world, and consequently the mission of the church. Others arise from a feeling of fear or inadequacy, or being overwhelmed by the problems. Perhaps the biggest barrier to many is a hectic lifestyle that leaves no room for these 'extra' concerns.

Of course, when asked directly, few Christians would deny that justice is an important issue. Responses will include comments such as, 'of course God cares about injustice ... but it is a distraction from preaching the gospel'; 'in an *ideal* world, there would be more justice in the world ... but we don't live in an ideal world'; 'justice is important ... but there are so many other things to do', etc. We need to carefully think about these 'buts'.

This chapter deals with the ten most common reasons for not getting involved in issues of injustice. It offers some preliminary thoughts on how to respond to each reason. Hopefully, this will whet your appetite for the fuller treatment of each issue in the rest of the book. The reasons are sometimes presented in stark terms to emphasise the essence of the argument. It is unlikely that you will identify personally with all of these reasons, but some are likely to strike a chord.

The Arguments Against Involvement

1. *It is a distraction from evangelism and therefore not a priority*

Argument
God's main concern is that people are saved (i.e. they repent of their sinful ways and accept Jesus as personal LORD and Saviour). Anything that takes time or effort away from this is a distraction from the true mission of God's people. In fact, involvement in issues of injustice in the past has led to a dilution of the gospel, as can be seen in the social gospel movement at the beginning of the twentieth century. We must therefore stick to preaching the 'gospel' so that as many people as possible are saved.

Possible answer (chapters 2–4)
It is true that God wants everyone to be saved. God wants everyone to recognise his or her need for him and enter into a relationship with him. Only in God can anyone find their true identity and purpose in this life, and receive eternal life. The church must preach this as its priority. However, God does not split people into physical, emotional, or spiritual parts but treats people as whole human beings. Jesus says, 'I have come that they may have life, and have it to the full' (Jn. 10:10). He is concerned about every aspect of our lives and he instructs his followers to be concerned with the whole person as well. Jesus does not hold evangelism and social action in tension with each other, but has an integral

approach, treating people as human beings and responding to every need (Lk. 8:40–56; Jn. 6). In his mission statement (Lk. 4:18–19), Jesus outlines a much fuller concept of the 'good news', including the release of prisoners, freedom for the oppressed, sight for the blind and the Year of Jubilee (Lev. 25), which focuses on bringing social justice to Israel by restoring people, land and wealth to how it was when the Israelites originally occupied the Promised Land.

The story of the Bible shows that God is planning the redemption and transformation of the whole of the world as he brings about his kingdom. It is not just spiritual transformation or personal transformation but Romans 8:21 says, 'the creation itself will be liberated from the its bondage to decay and brought into the glorious freedom of the children of God'. The good news of the kingdom is good news to human beings in all their fullness, so social justice must be an integral part of the mission of God's people.

2. *Jesus was not political so we should not be either*

Argument
Jesus was not a member of any political party, and there is no New Testament reference to any political activity, so we cannot get involved in politics. To do so would be outside Jesus' calling. In fact, political activity is distinctly 'unchristian'.

Possible answer (chapter 5)
If politics is about the use of power at all levels of society to bring about change, then Jesus was certainly political. Although he was not a member of any political party and did not hold any official position of power, Jesus challenged the corruption, hypocrisy and injustice in Jewish society. For example, he turned over the tables in the Temple (Mk. 11:15–17); he warned the people to be careful about the

teaching of the Pharisees (Mt. 16:6); and he rebuked the Pharisees for their neglect of justice (Mt. 23:23). In fact, it could be argued that the Jewish leaders decided to kill Jesus because he was political and challenged their power and authority over the people of Palestine (Lk. 20:19).

However, Jesus' approach to power and politics was different from those around him. He modelled servant leadership (Jn. 13), was humble, and associated with those on the edges of society (e.g. the Samaritan woman at the well, Jn. 4:1–26). Jesus was a revolutionary: he taught love for enemies (Mt. 5:44), he did not use force to bring change (Jn. 18:36) and was prepared to suffer rather than cause suffering (Mt. 8:17). Yet, Jesus was political because he did not just sit back and allow others to dictate how the world would be. He was determined to transform the world.

In a democracy, we make a political decision if we refuse to do anything to get involved because our response is an approval of things as they are, however unjust they may be.

3. Romans 13 tells us we need to obey the state so we cannot criticise their actions

Argument
Romans 13:1–2 says 'Everyone must submit himself to the governing authorities, for there is no authority except that which God has established … he who rebels against the authority is rebelling against what God has instituted.' This means that God appoints all authorities and by challenging authority we are challenging what God has put in place. By criticising the government of the day we are also disobeying the command to submit. Furthermore, Jesus says, 'Give to Caesar what is Caesar's and to God what is God's'(Mk. 12:17). This implies a due respect for and cooperation with the authorities, which allows no room for opposition.

Possible answer (chapter 3)

Government is good and a part of God's plan. However, creation, human beings and government are now affected by sin. Although government still has a role, it is limited because of its fallen state. Romans 13 indicates that the main role of government is to judge and punish evil; administer justice and protect the weak; and promote human well-being. When Paul was writing his letter to the Christians in Rome, they were able to live in relative peace and could obey the state and still be faithful to God's laws. This is not always the case because the state is affected by individual and institutional sin and can be profoundly corrupted (Rev. 18). Such authority cannot be respected as the righteous instrument of God, so he commands his disciples to 'Come out of her ... so that you will not share in her sins' (Rev. 18:4).

Romans 13 is also about mutual responsibilities (i.e. the responsibilities of governments to govern in the way God intended, and the responsibilities of people to be good citizens). Therefore, submission to the state doesn't mean uncritical obedience. Paul showed this when he challenged the authorities in Philippi for having him beaten and unjustly imprisoned, thus denying him his rights as a Roman citizen (Acts 16). Paul and Silas also carried on preaching the good news, even though they had been told by the authorities to stop (Acts 17:6–7). We are therefore given the choice to obey the state when it is acting in line with God's will, or to challenge the state when it is out of line. History shows that when the church and state have been too close (e.g. during the reign of the Emperor Constantine, in the Crusades, in Nazi Germany, or, more recently, in Rwanda), the church has lost its prophetic ministry and allowed abuses of power.

4. There are two kingdoms – the kingdom of God and the kingdom of this world. As Christians we live in the kingdom of God and that is our focus

Argument
There are two distinct kingdoms – the kingdom of God that deals with spiritual matters, and the kingdom of the world that deals with worldly matters. The two spheres have little overlap and the church, firmly placed in the kingdom of God, should leave worldly matters to the state. The only time the church needs to engage with the state is when state actions prevent it from operating freely by restricting worship or evangelism.

Possible answer (chapters 2–4)
It is true that there are two kingdoms but as Christians we belong to the kingdom of God and we live in the kingdom of this world. Our citizenship is of heaven (Phil. 3:20). That is our home and to where we owe our primary allegiance. However, we are also citizens of the earth and we have responsibility to our fellow citizens (Jn. 17:13–19).

We need to recognise that the authorities are ordained by God and are his servants to do good and to punish evil. We can hold the state to account if it is neglecting to act in the way God intended it to act. Usually, this neglect will involve abuse of power in oppressing people or withholding justice. To ignore such neglect is to affirm evil and deny the heavenly kingdom to which Christians belong.

We are called to love our neighbour as ourselves (Mt. 6:20). When we have the opportunity, we should 'do good to all people' (Gal. 6:9). We will not be able to do this if we opt out of society. When Jesus prays for his disciples, he clearly expects them to remain in the world and bring about change (Jn. 17:14–18). Jesus says his kingdom was not *of* the world, but he never says his kingdom wasn't *in* the world. In fact, Jesus says Christians are 'the salt of the earth and the light of the world' (Mt. 5:13–16). It is difficult to imagine how Christians could be preserving and illuminating agents without being in close contact with the world.

5. Injustice is part of the way things are. The world will get worse until Jesus returns and will then be destroyed

Argument
We are in the last days between Jesus' first and second coming. The world is going to get worse before Jesus returns. He will then destroy the world and create a new one. In the meantime, it is futile to fight against the inevitability of oppression and injustice; it is simply the way things have to be. It is all part of God's plan. To emphasise this Jesus says in Mark 14:7, 'the poor you will always have with you'. In fact, to fight injustice may even slow down Jesus' return.

Possible answer (chapter 2)
The physical universe is not destined for destruction but for renewal (Mt. 19:28; Acts 3:21; Rom. 8:19–21). The world we live in is not evil, but is fallen and will be redeemed. It will be transformed and there will be a 'new heaven and a new earth'. 'The holy city, the new Jerusalem' will come down out of heaven and God will 'make his dwelling with men' (Rev. 21:1–3). This means that 'the kingdom of the world will become the kingdom of our LORD ... and he will reign for ever' (Rev. 11:5). So the current world will be transformed and God's kingdom will come. His will is going to be done on earth as it is in heaven.

Jesus made it clear that he inaugurated the kingdom (Mk. 1:15) and that it is growing (Mt. 12:28). However, we have to wait until the second coming for its fulfilment (Mk. 4:19;

Rev. 11:5). Satan is already defeated, but his final destruction is not yet. Meanwhile, there is a battle raging in the kingdom of the world, because the coming of the kingdom of God produces opposition. We will see signs of God's kingdom and signs of the kingdom of the world. They will be in opposition to each other.

Oppression and injustice will be present because Satan is allowed to have limited rule on the earth. However, God speaks out strongly against these. Justice is at the heart of his character (Dt. 10:18) and he commands us to be just. He frequently sent prophets to denounce the idolatry of his people, and the subsequent injustice within Israelite society (Isa. 58; Amos 5). The Proverbs exhort us to 'speak up and judge fairly; defend the rights of the poor and the needy' (Prov. 31:9). Jesus stresses that concern for the poor and justice is central to his ministry. He uses the example of the Good Samaritan to show what loving one's neighbour looks like in practice. He rebuked the Pharisees for neglecting justice (Mt. 23:23; Lk. 11:42).

When Jesus says 'the poor are always with you' (Mk. 14:7), he adds, 'so you can always help them'. It is a not a call to ignore their needs but to meet them.

6. It is a spiritual battle and therefore spiritual warfare is the answer

Argument
The reason this world is in such a mess is that we are engaged in a spiritual battle. Ephesians 6:12 says, 'our struggle is not against flesh and blood, but against the rulers, against the authorities, against the powers of this dark world and against the spiritual forces of evil in the heavenly realms'. We therefore have to fight injustice on the spiritual level, binding demons, bringing down strongholds and engaging in spiritual warfare. Tackling the government or

fighting injustice on a practical level will not get to the root of the problem and will therefore bring little change.

Possible answer (chapter 4)
It is true that the systems and structures of the world are fallen (Rom. 8:20–21), people are fallen (Rom. 3:23), and those with authority tend towards abusing their power (Mt. 20:25; Rev. 18). We are engaged in a spiritual battle and prayer is a vital weapon in our fight against injustice. In fact, without prayer, our actions will have only limited impact and may even be futile.

However, we are also called to take action. We are called to be salt and light (Mt. 5:13–16), which means becoming involved in society to bring about change and also speaking out and showing society the truth. The mission of the church involves being a positive influence in society to bring its laws and actions more in line with God's will for the world. We are called to love our neighbours as ourselves (Mt. 6:10), which means ensuring they have food, clothes and shelter. It also means treating the poor with special concern (Jas. 2:1–13) and working for justice (Mt. 23:23).

7. *Politics is a dirty game and will compromise those who are involved*

Argument
Politics is about compromise. In politics you need to come to an agreement with many different people, representing different concerns and as a Christian you will not be able to hold true to your Christian beliefs. You will have to compromise and you will undermine your witness and cause others to stumble. Also, power corrupts and many politicians are only involved for personal gain or to protect a narrow group of interests. It will be almost impossible for a Christian to retain any distinctiveness. When Christians

or the church have become involved in politics in the past, it has only caused problems and damaged the church's reputation.

Possible answer (chapters 3, 6, 10 & 15)
Political involvement is much wider than just being elected as an MP or holding political office. Political activity involves engaging at all levels of society to bring about change, and to bring a society more in line with God's will. If Christians are not involved in political activity then this just leaves all decisions about how a country is run to those who do not recognise the Lordship of Christ.

Holding political office or being in a position of influence can be very challenging for those who want to live lives of integrity. However, it is also a great opportunity for effective Christian witness. Those who remain above reproach and conduct themselves with integrity will win the respect of others. To do this they will need the support of other Christians who can pray with them, hold them to account and offer them wise counsel. However, Christians are often the most critical of other Christians making a stand to try and bring change.

Finally, if the church has become involved in the past and been compromised, lessons need to be learned so the church can take its rightful place. But there are also many examples from all over the world where Christians and the church as an institution have engaged and brought significant change. Some of these are included in chapters 7–12.

8. It is all too complicated and I won't be able to make a difference

Argument
There are too many issues to deal with. In my town there are high levels of unemployment, racial discrimination,

people living on the street and children denied access to an education. People all over the world are unjustly imprisoned; others are forcibly removed from their land or are in slavery; unpayable debt is crippling many countries' economies; Christians are being persecuted for their beliefs, etc. There are too many problems that are all connected in some way. The situation is complicated. I don't know where to start. Furthermore, I don't see what difference one person can make in the face of all of these problems.

Possible answer (chapters 9, 12–14)
It is true that in an increasingly interconnected world, not only are we more aware of problems that exist, but the problems seem to be more complicated. However, instead of trying to understand and solve everything at once, it is good to start with a manageable task. First, pray that God will guide you in how to become involved. Then select one issue and find out more about it. Next, try and join with those who are already doing something about it. By working with others you can pool skills, hone a strategy and receive support and encouragement. Make sure you also stay involved. Keep a track of what you have done, and keep up to date on the situation so that you will know what difference your actions are making. The stories in this book show that individuals can make a difference and are even more effective when working together with others. A few concerned individuals soon mount a significant force for change.

You could also encourage your home group to start studying biblical passages on justice and to support each other in making small steps to see justice done. This could help your local church to become more involved.

9. *It is too risky*

Argument
I live in a country with an authoritarian government that puts down any dissent with violence. The church struggles each year to be recognised as legitimate and to register to be able to operate. We cannot do anything that will put our chances of meeting together in jeopardy. Also, it is far too dangerous. Others have been falsely imprisoned or have disappeared. My family may be targeted and I would not be willing to put them through that. Also, if something did happen to me, who would look after them?

Possible answer (chapters 7, 9–11)
Standing up for justice can be dangerous, especially when standing against people or systems that are abusing their power. Any decision to become involved should not be taken lightly. In such situations you are unlikely to be able to remove all risk, but will be able to reduce it. Work in a network because there is strength in numbers. Ensure you know your rights and make contacts with lawyers and human rights groups who will be able to give professional help. Build relationships with groups outside of the country who may be able to influence the government or authority from outside. Build contacts with those in power, who may be able to help you if you are in trouble. If you think that a threat to your family, friends or colleagues is a possibility, discuss the issues with them, pray with them and come to a joint decision about what you will do. Regularly review the situation to see if anything has changed.

In a situation when challenging the government is difficult, you may take an alternative approach of building up good will. If you are working for a development organisation where you know that your project has a good model for, say, providing healthcare to the whole community, or building up local business skills, then this information is likely to be useful to the government. Governments are dependent on the knowledge of people with grassroots experience, to help them develop effective policies that will work for the country.

Also, it may be that you decide acting is too dangerous. If this is the case, consider passing on information to groups outside the country who could act on your behalf.

10. *To be honest, I have too many problems of my own and not enough time*

Argument
Life is difficult. I struggle to keep my head above water managing a family/going to work/being involved in church/keeping in touch with friends and family/earning enough money. I do not have the energy to worry about other people's problems as well as my own. I know there are problems in the world and others are worse off than me, but it would just be one thing too much to become involved. I need to guard my free time so that I have some space for God and myself.

Possible answer (chapters 2–3, 13–14)
Some people's lives are more difficult than others. We all have different responsibilities in our lives, and some people seem to have very little free time after fulfilling these. Each situation is different, but I would offer three possible lines of action. First, pray for God's compassion and wisdom. If you are reading this, it is likely that you want to get more involved. God promises us his Holy Spirit to guide us in all truth (Jn. 14:15–27) and to give us compassionate hearts (Ezek. 36:26). Secondly, make contact with people who are suffering or worse off than you in some way. It is through seeing people who are oppressed or suffering injustice that

we learn to see them as individuals, not as faceless statistics. Thirdly, take some time to look at your life and your priorities. Are you happy with this? It may be that you are happy and feel no call to change. However, it may just be that you will come to see that God is asking you to get involved and to start working for his justice.

Conclusion

Whatever the reasons for lack of involvement, we need to be as honest as possible about the barriers to overcome, individually, as churches and as Christian organisations. This will help us to move forward and be more faithful servants. If we have sinned through lack of involvement, we need to seek God's forgiveness. The Bible promises that, 'If we confess our sins, he is faithful and just and will forgive us our sins and purify us from all unrighteousness' (1 Jn. 1:9).

However, God does not want us to be paralysed by guilt. He wants us to be liberated by his grace, freed from sin and changed to become more like him. He promises us his Holy Spirit for this task, 'if you love me, you will obey what I command. And I will ask the Father, and he will give you another Counsellor to be with you forever – the Spirit of truth' (Jn. 14:15–17). This book aims to help each one of us reach a deeper understanding of God's concern for justice and to consider what could happen if we got involved.

Questions for Reflection

• Which of the reasons do you most identify with and why?
• Are you persuaded by the answers suggested?
• What questions and concerns do you still need to address?

- Which chapters in the book look most useful to you? Consider reading those first.
- Who can help you work through some of the issues as you read through the book?

2

The Kingdom of God and the Mission of the Church

Introduction

In order to understand why involvement in issues of social justice is important it is necessary to get a better understanding of the mission of the church in society. As shown below, the mission of the church is to work with God to bring about his kingdom. The kingdom of God is one of the central themes of the Bible. It is therefore as good a place as any to start in order to understand what plans God has for his world and where justice fits in.

The Kingdom of God

According to Kraybill,

> Most biblical scholars agree that the kingdom of God means the dynamic rule or reign of God. The reign of God represents God's government, authority, and ruling power ... the kingdom is present whenever and wherever women and men submit their lives to God's authority.[1]

This includes in people's hearts, relationships, systems and structures. History can be seen as God's story of establishing his kingdom, told in the Bible by God himself. It is a story in which his people have cooperated at times, and in which we can choose to cooperate.

The phrase 'the kingdom of God' is virtually absent from the Old Testament although the concept of kingship and God's sovereignty or rule is everywhere. God is constantly calling on his people to give the honour and worship that is due to their King. His sovereignty stretches throughout the earth because God has power over all earthly kings (Isa. 40:23), although he allows them to rule over their territories. Isaiah looks forward to a future kingdom in which the Messiah will reign and put all things right and bring blessing to his people (Isa. 61:1–4, 65:17–25).

The kingdom of God (or kingdom of Heaven in Matthew's Gospel) is the most frequently mentioned topic in the Gospels. Being 'born of the spirit' (Jn 3:5), receiving eternal life and entering the kingdom of God are in fact the same things, expressed in different ways.

However, the kingdom is not everywhere and another kingdom, the kingdom of this world, has been set up in direct opposition to God's kingdom. Satan and other angelic powers have seceded from God's rule and have drawn humankind into the rebellion. God has already won the final victory through Jesus' death on the cross (1 Cor. 15:54–55), but this victory will only be fully consummated when Christ returns (Rev. 11:15) and God's reign will be complete. We need to keep the fact of this final victory in mind as we approach the reality of the world that we live in. We need to look beyond the immediate world that we see to the spiritual reality behind it and also to the all-powerful God who is in control and is working his purposes out. This gives us hope for the future, which provides the motivations for current actions.

Focusing on the kingdom of God enables us to understand the wider implications of Jesus' life, death and resurrection. He has come to restore all things to how they should be, to tackle the effects of all sin, which includes offering individual salvation as well as restoration of our society.

Jesus and the Kingdom

John the Baptist preached that this kingdom was near, so by the time Jesus came, the Jewish people were full of expectation. However, they had a very different kingdom in mind, a political kingdom that would overthrow the Romans and re-establish the Jews as rulers of their land. Jesus began his public ministry by announcing 'the kingdom of God is at hand, repent and believe the good news!' (Mk. 1:15). Jesus does not give us a definition of the kingdom; perhaps the closest we get is in the LORD's Prayer, 'Your kingdom come, your will be done on earth as it is in heaven' (Mt. 6:10). Some of the most significant aspects of the kingdom are highlighted below.

Jesus brings in the kingdom

Jesus told his followers that the signs he did were a demonstration that the kingdom of God had come upon them (Mt. 12:28), although they had to make the choice about whether or not to enter. Jesus brought about the kingdom of God in person, through his obedience to God, through the signs he performed and, supremely, through his death and resurrection. The offer of salvation is extended to all people who humbly submit to the Lordship of Christ, for he is the only way to enter the kingdom and be saved (Jn 14:6). Deciding to enter the kingdom and be saved is the most important choice that anyone has to make, as it brings us from death to life (1 Jn. 3:14) and is to be sought above all things (Mt. 6:33).

The kingdom has come but we await its fulfilment

It has penetrated the present in the person of Jesus, but will only be fulfilled in the future. Jesus talks of the age to come (Mk. 4:19) and the close of this age when the Son of Man comes to judge humanity (Mt. 13:37–43). We see many signs of the kingdom now, but the full glory is yet to be revealed, and awaits the second coming of Christ (Rev. 11:15). When this happens the earth will be transformed. The physical universe is destined for renewal, not destruction (Mt. 19:28; Acts 3:21; Rom. 8:19–21), because we do not live in an evil world, but a corrupted or fallen one. There will be a new heaven and a new earth, and the new Jerusalem will come down out of heaven and God will make his dwelling with men (Rev. 21:1–3). So the current world will be transformed and the LORD's Prayer fulfilled because God's kingdom will have come and his will be done on earth as in heaven. Keeping this in mind gives us hope that God's will is going to be done on earth, but also helps us to be realistic about how much will change before Jesus comes again.

The kingdom is not an earthly political entity

When Pilate questioned Jesus about his political ambitions, Jesus told him that his kingship would not manifest itself like a human kingdom (Jn. 18:36). It is not taken by force (Lk. 4:1–13). Rather, suffering, denial and service, as shown by Jesus' death on the cross, are at the heart of God's kingdom. Jesus said his kingdom was not *of* this world, but he didn't say his kingdom wasn't *in* it. According to Kraybill:

Jesus didn't plead for withdrawal. Nor does he assume that kingdom and world are divided neatly into separate realms. Kingdom action takes place in the middle of the societal ballpark. But it's a different game. Kingdom players follow new rules. They listen to another coach. Kingdom values challenge patterns of social life taken for granted in modern culture.[2]

The kingdom provokes opposition

When confronted with the kingdom of God, some will seek humbly to enter it and be saved, but it often excites hostility. Rejection of the kingdom and all it stands for is part of a wider battle where Satan and his allies strive relentlessly to thwart, corrupt and rival God's kingdom. Persecution is a hallmark of Christians of this age (2 Tim. 3:12), although it will be absent from the age to come (Rev. 21:4). This means that those who are, for example, preaching the gospel, caring for those in need, working towards justice and challenging oppression are likely to come across opposition. It can be costly to break the power of evil, but God is with us, and we know he has the ultimate victory. If we get involved he will give us everything we need.

Entering the kingdom produces a reformed character

The character of the kingdom is the character of God the Father, Son and Holy Spirit. This means citizens call the King their father and share in his riches. Central to the kingdom is grace: God's grace to us in Jesus and our grace to others in the power of the indwelling Spirit. The Beatitudes (Mt. 5:3–10) further outline characteristics of God's people: to be poor in spirit, to hunger and thirst for righteousness and justice, to be merciful and to be peacemakers. This character enables Christians to be the 'salt and light' of the earth and enables others to experience the goodness of the kingdom and to enter it for themselves. We are required to have a character consistent with the message we preach. As a Christian community we can encourage each other towards holiness and obedience.

The kingdom will bring shalom

Central to the good news of the gospel is the idea of restoring things to how God originally intended or redeeming things for their original purpose (Col. 1:20). There will be redemption and reconciliation. This redemption, brought about by Jesus' life, death and resurrection, enables individuals to be redeemed to live in a relationship with God, but it is wider than that. The kingdom of God is a new order that is being brought about on earth. God has a plan to make his world more like he wants it to be. That includes changing people so that they are reconciled with him and grow in his likeness, but is also means changing the political, social and economic systems and structures – so that they act in line with his will. Nothing is outside of the reach of the kingdom and he will leave nothing untouched. Jesus has also brought all powers under his control; so another sign of the good news of the kingdom will be structures and systems being redeemed for their original purposes (Rev. 11:15). Changing people is essential, but it is not enough. According to one commentator:

> There are entrenched powers and monstrous structures we need to address and contend with. There is such a thing as organised injustice, which calls for thoughtful social analysis and complex solutions ... unjust social structures require more than the presence of changed individuals. Evangelism is not a cure-all, and cannot substitute for concrete redemptive action in our political and social life.[3]

Shalom

The kingdom of God is characterised by *shalom*, a Hebrew word meaning, amongst other things, social justice, peace and prosperity. *Shalom* means well-being, in the widest sense of the word. It is first and foremost a declaration about right relationships, indicating that injustice, and lack of peace and prosperity are due to broken relationships between people and God and between each other. Prophesies about Jesus the Messiah talk about him establishing an age of *shalom*, characterised by his just and liberating rule:

'For unto us a child is born, to us a son is given, and the government will be on his shoulders. And he will be called Wonderful Counsellor, Mighty God, Everlasting Father, *Prince of Peace*. Of the increase of his government and peace there will be no end. He will reign on David's throne and over his kingdom, establishing and upholding it with justice and righteousness from that time on and for ever' (Isa. 9:6–7).

It is good news to the poor

Jesus announces his mission in the synagogue in Capernaum by quoting from Isaiah 61:

The Spirit of the LORD is on me, because he has anointed me to preach good news to the poor. He has sent me to proclaim freedom for the prisoners and recovery of sight for the blind, to release the oppressed, to proclaim the year of the LORD's favour…and he began by saying to them 'today this Scripture is fulfilled in your hearing' (Lk. 4:18–19; 21).

Most commentators agree that the year of the LORD's favour in Isaiah 61 is referring to the Jubilee (Lev. 25) when after every fifty years slaves should be freed, debts forgiven, land and property returned to its original owners and the land should lie fallow. It was a year of liberation for the Hebrew community. It recognised that injustices would enter the covenant community. It makes the point that it is God, not the people, who own their land, and it gives people back their dignity by enabling the poor to meet their own needs. The ram's horn was blown on the Day of Atonement (*Yom Kippur*), when the community had been put right with God. The Jubilee laws then ensured they were right with one another.

The purpose of the Jubilee law was to restore things to how they were when Israel first entered the Promised Land when everyone had enough land, everyone was free, people lived in their clans and families and the land was fertile. It was *shalom* in action. By announcing that Isaiah 61:1–2 was fulfilled in their hearing, Jesus said that his kingdom was a kingdom of Jubilee principles, to be enacted not only once every fifty years, but from then onwards. Justice for all was to be a central part of his kingdom and that kingdom is now!

Here 'release' (for the oppressed) translates the Greek *aphesis*, which is the key New Testament word for forgiveness. It is therefore clear that the release Jesus talks about is meant in a spiritual sense and that he is declaring that he can release people from sin. However, it is not just spiritual freedom because Jesus died and rose to release people from all effects of sin. The Jubilee law focuses on releasing people from all that prevents them living life to the full and from experiencing God's *shalom*. We need to see his mission statement as referring to the fullness of salvation.

Another sign of the kingdom is healing. When John asked if Jesus was the one to expect, he replied: 'tell him what you have seen and heard. The lame walk, the sick are healed' (Mt. 11:4–5).

This is good news for everyone, but especially for the poor. In the Bible, the word 'poor' refers to two groups of people: those who are economically and socially poor, who suffered injustice and oppression (see chapter 3), and those who humbly trust God (Ps. 86:1–2).

The focus of this book is on the first group. The kingdom of God is especially good news for them because they suffer the most under unjust rulers, they are often politically weak and are denied justice (Ecc. 4:1). They are often dependent on others for their food, shelter and security. The poor are seen as nobodies in society and overlooked or even looked down upon. They are denied the social justice of *shalom* and the opportunity to have material sufficiency to live life to the full. So it is especially good news for them because Jesus' kingdom turns the world's values upside down. For the poor, *shalom* means improved economic, social, political and spiritual life, although it may involve persecution as well. In this present age this redemption will always be partial, but the final consummation at Jesus' second coming is certain. We are called to work with God to make this 'good news to the poor' a reality in this world.

Those who are poor also have a special place in God's plan: 'has not God chosen those who are poor in the eyes of the world to be rich in faith and inherit the kingdom he promised to those who love him?' (Jas. 2:5). God chooses to pour out his blessings on the weak and powerless and he uses the poor to bring about his plans of salvation.

So, as God is bringing about his kingdom, what is the role of his people? In other words, what is the mission of the church?

The Mission of the Church

As men and women submit to the rule of Jesus and enter into the blessings of the kingdom, they are gathered into the fellowship of the church. The church is the people of God, called out of the world, called to God and gathered together to work with God to fulfil his purpose in bringing about his kingdom. The church is therefore a visible sign of the outworking of the kingdom of God here on earth. It brings the good news to all people.

There is only one church, only one people of God, but it has many different forms. The word for church in the New Testament is *ekklesia* and means simply 'a gathering of people'. It is used to describe a local gathering of Christians (1 Thes. 1:1), the gathering of all the Christians in the world (Gal. 1:13), small house gatherings (Rom. 16:5), a Hebrew congregation in Jerusalem and a Gentile congregation in Antioch, and a number of separate Christian communities in distinct localities (Acts 15:41).

Over the centuries what is known as church has come to include all sorts of different institutions, denominations and even buildings, but through it all the New Testament reality has persisted. So, groups of people that are devoted to Jesus, to each other and to serving their neighbour can be found in different places. They can be an individual congregation or linked to a denomination such as the Anglican Church; within Christian development organisations; or simply a group of Christians who have come together with a common concern. One of the strengths of the church is that it operates at all different levels and can influence all levels of society. It is therefore vital that each expression of the church is connected with the wider body of believers for support, for accountability and for working together effectively to bring change.

When talking about the mission of the church, we are looking at the church in all its forms as a gathered community of believers. It is important to note that the institutional church is only one form of church and God uses all forms to bring about his kingdom. He uses individual Christians with individual ministries (e.g. a Christian politician); he uses group of people who get together for a ministry (e.g. who visit elderly people in a community); and he uses Christian organisations (e.g. who defend human rights of those wrongly imprisoned). In his sovereignty, God also intervenes directly and uses those who do not recognise his rule (e.g. Nebuchadnezzar).

Paul gives us the powerful image of the church as the body of Christ: 'God has arranged the parts of the body, every one of them, just as he wanted them to be ... so there should be no division in the body' (1 Cor. 12:12–31). The main point of the passage is that every part of the body of Christ should be working with every other part, not only to support each other, but also to ensure that ministry is more effective. Therefore gifts of administration, service and hospitality, which are often seen as inferior gifts, need to be recognised as enabling the church to fulfil its mission. They need to be recognised as much as some of the more public and high-profile gifts such as teaching, prophesy and healing. The body of Christ will not function unless each person's gifts are supported and developed. This is part of discipleship and living as a kingdom people.

So, the mission of the church is to work with God to extend his rule over every aspect of people's lives. What does this mean in practice? Instead of trying to offer a watertight definition of what this might mean, I suggest below a list of activities or functions that this might include. These are based on an understanding of how God brings about his kingdom and are in no particular order. Some of these activities will be undertaken by individuals, others by small gatherings of believers and still others by the church as an institution.

However, even when individuals with particular gifts undertake some of the work (e.g. standing for political office, running a project to befriend refugees), they will still need the support of the church in prayer and encouragement in their work. In many ways it is still the local church as an institution that is undertaking the work as part of its mission, even though only a few people from the congregation are practically involved. This principle is the same in the more 'spiritual' callings (e.g. we all need to evangelise but some are evangelists and the job of the rest of the church is to support them in prayer, etc.). The tragedy is that many churches value the evangelist much more than those working for social justice and ignore Paul's emphasis on valuing all the gifts. Consequently they undermine the evangelistic impact of the church.

The mission of the church in practice

Worshipping God as his people	Being a people that give God his rightful honour.
Proclaiming the good news	Preaching the gospel so that people may turn to Christ and be saved from their sins.
Prayer for God to intervene	Part of the priestly role of interceding for the world. It also includes listening to God.
Discipleship	Helping others to grow in maturity in their faith through teaching, exercising gifts and pastoral support. Developing a godly character.
Caring for the needy and suffering	Being with people in time of need (e.g. sharing possessions, caring for the sick, visiting those living alone).
Stewardship	Looking after the environment, using money wisely and ensuring power is used well.
Modelling an alternative	Not opting out of the world, but modelling a different way of life and being a light to the world.
Prophetic role	Speaking out against idolatry and injustice, in the tradition of the Old Testament prophets and of Jesus himself.
Social action	Engaging with a society to carry on God's creative and redemptive acts, being salt to the world.

Social justice	Engaging with the powers of the day to hold them to account and bring their actions more in line with God's will.
Participation in institutions	Seeking political office or a position of responsibility in order to bring influence and change actions and policies.
Peace and reconciliation	This includes peace with God, with others and with God's creation.
Confronting the unseen powers	Some men and women are held directly by demons that possess them, others are held by sickness and the dread of death, which the evil powers exploit, others by the unjust structures that have evil powers behind them.
Signs and wonders	Demonstrating God's power and bringing healing.

Fulfilling the Whole Mission

None of these functions can be isolated from one another. They are all inseparably linked so for the church to fulfil its whole mission, it should be involved in all of them. Many churches have focused almost exclusively on the activities nearer the top of the list such as evangelism, prayer and discipleship. Others have concentrated on confronting the unseen powers and performing signs and wonders. Still others have focused primarily on social action and social justice. A narrow focus for mission will result in only a partial fulfilment of the role of the church in bringing the good news. As God's people we need to be faithful to the whole of our calling, not just the bits we like or find easiest.

All mission roles of the church have the same function, namely, bringing good news to all people, especially the poor. If the church neglects these social justice roles, we are being unfaithful to our calling. Conversely, if the church only concentrates on these, we are being unfaithful to our overall mission. Social justice is therefore a key part of the mission of the church, but it is only one part, and needs to be integrated with the rest.

The church needs to be both a herald of the good news and a sign that the kingdom has come. It needs to be both prophetic in showing what is wrong with the world, and practical in offering alternatives. To do this, Christians need to form strong communities of believers that engage as stewards in all that God has created.

With this understanding, this book focuses on the role of the church in challenging injustice and oppression and bringing social change in society, often through individual members or groups of members. This justice is to be God's justice, based on the guidance we receive from his word. The main areas to focus on from the above table are therefore seeking social justice, participating in institutions, a prophetic role in speaking out, seeking peace and reconciliation, and praying for God to intervene. To be effective, these will need to be closely linked to, and backed up by the other activities, such as caring for those in need and proclamation of the good news. As seen from the case studies in chapters 7–12, often these actions are all going on at once.

Influencing local development priorities, Camborne, UK

Camborne in Cornwall had been highlighted as an area of deprivation, so there are various government schemes with money available for local development work. The local Elim Church applied for money from one scheme, but was turned down. On further investigation, Mike Hooper, the minister of the church, found that the government bodies tended to be suspicious of any faith-based organisations involved in social provision and that most Christian organisations were suspicious of working with secular groups, whether they were the government or businesses.

An opportunity came to try and bridge this divide. The local authority set up a Local Strategic Partnership (LSP), which is a forum for statutory bodies, local business and voluntary sector organisations to get together and plan the development of the local district. As the religious organisations were the main social providers behind the government, Mike lobbied for a Faith Community Representation to be on this Partnership, as per government guidelines. He was successful and is now the representative himself. Of his hopes he says, 'The LSP covers issues such as crime prevention, housing, education and community networks. The church has something to say on all of these issues. Christians can apply theological principles to a sociological context, especially the idea of community and care. For example, we have suggested to the police that faith groups can be a part of the support package for someone who has just finished probation, provided that person is an active member of the group. The statutory authorities still have the primary role but we can have a supporting role. We want to influence policy and also to change the perception of what faith based organisations can do. I hope that Christians will get involved in the sub-committees on different issues so that a Christian ethos and ethics can be at the forefront of the implementation of social policy.'

The local churches have been encouraged by the work of the local Elim church and most of the churches in Camborne are looking at how they can be more involved in social action.

The Bible also says that tackling oppression and seeking social justice will lead to a more effective witness and that God promises that through these actions his light will shine forth:

> Is this not the kind of fasting I have chosen:
> to loose the chains of injustice and untie the cords of the yoke,
> to set the oppressed free and break every yoke?
> Is it not to share your food with the hungry,
> and to provide the poor wanderer with shelter –

when you see the naked, to clothe him,
and not to turn away from your own flesh and blood?
Then your light will break forth like the dawn,
and your healing will quickly appear;
then your righteousness will go before you,
and the glory of the LORD will be your rearguard.

(Isa. 58:6–8)

Questions for Reflection

- What difference does it make to the way you live your life if you believe that God's kingdom has already come, even though we await its final fulfilment?
- What is the connection between the kingdom of God and the mission of the church? What are the implications of this for your church?
- How would you explain the links between social involvement and evangelism?
- What activities does your church spend most time doing? Is there anything you think needs to change?
- What could happen if you got involved in your local community?

Further Reading

Ellul, Jacques, *The Presence of the Kingdom*
Goldsworthy, Graeme, *Gospel and Kingdom*
Hughes, Dewi and Matthew Bennett, *God of the Poor*
Kraybill, Donald B., *The Upside-down Kingdom*
Maggay, Melba Padilla, *Transforming Society*
Stevens, R. Paul, *The Abolition of the Laity: Vocation, Work and Ministry in a Biblical Perspective*

3

Poverty, Justice and the State

God's Concern for the Poor

As we saw in the previous chapter, the kingdom of God is good news to the poor. In the Bible, the word 'poor' refers to two groups of people: those who are economically or socially poor and those who are spiritually poor and humbly submit themselves to God.

The spiritually poor are those who recognise their dependence on God and make themselves available to be used by him to further his purposes (2 Cor. 4:7). In Matthew 5:3, when Jesus says 'blessed are the poor in spirit', he is referring to those who humbly submit themselves to God.

The materially poor are generally those who cannot meet their basic needs, including adequate food, shelter, healthcare and means of production. In the Bible the poor are generally those without land or without any means of supporting themselves (e.g. widows and orphans). They suffer oppression by the rich (Isa. 58; Amos 2:6–7; 5), and are marginalised and powerless (Ecc. 4:1).

In this book, poor refers to the first group – those who are on the margins of society, who are excluded in some way, who are denied basic needs and basic rights or who suffer injustice. The good news of the gospel is directed towards the poor because when Christians live lives that demonstrate *shalom* (e.g. through sharing their food and belongings with the poor, seeking justice, defending the rights of the oppressed and helping those in need) the poor will benefit and experience some of God's blessing.

So, apart from the kingdom of God being good news to the poor, how does God see them?

Made in God's image

The starting point has to be the fact that all human beings are made in God's image (Gen. 1:26–27) and are loved by him. They therefore have equal value and should have equal respect for one another.

God loves us all so much that Jesus came down to earth as a man. Through his incarnation, Jesus identified with us in our weakness and poverty (Phil. 2:6–11). He left the glory and richness of heaven to be born to an artisan family in the social backwater of Galilee. He submitted himself completely to the will of his Father (Mt. 26:42) and he became poor so that we may become rich and have eternal life (2 Cor. 8:9).

Focus of God's concern

God's love for human beings involves a special concern for those who are poor, marginalised and oppressed. He hates it when people suffer or are oppressed. It is an insult to him (Prov. 14:31). Those who oppress the poor will be punished (Isa. 10:1–2).

Jesus announced that he came to bring 'good news to the poor' (Lk. 4:18–19) and his ministry was towards the marginalised in society. He was accused of associating with 'tax-collectors and sinners' (Lk. 5:30–31); he accepted anointing by a 'sinful woman' (Lk. 7:36–50); he encouraged children to be brought to him (Lk. 18:16); and he went

out of his way to speak to the Samaritan woman at the well
(Jn. 4:1–26).

Time and again God selects the weak and the powerless
upon whom to pour out his blessings and through whom to
fulfil his purposes (1 Cor. 1:26–19; Jas. 2:1–7). To be faithful to our calling, we also need to have a special concern for
the poor and to focus our mission on the margins, which
others have forgotten or neglected.

In need of salvation

However, we also need to remember that 'the poor' are individual people. Like all other people, they are sinful, and in
need of salvation. There is a danger in either romanticising
their situation or treating them as a homogenous group.
They are

> people of flesh and blood like ourselves – made in the image of
> God; sinful and in need of restoring their relationship to God,
> to neighbour, and to creation; loved by God in Jesus Christ and
> with the potential to become partners with God in the fulfil-
> ment of his purpose for humankind and for creation.[1]

Denied basic needs

Jesus uses the example of the Good Samaritan to help us
understand how to love our neighbour (Lk. 10:25–17) and
ensure their needs are met. He does not leave it as an option
to ignore those in need. Jesus assumes that caring for the
poor is a part of everyday Christian living – 'when you give
to the needy …' (Mt. 6:2). We will always be called to serve
the poor. As Jesus said, 'the poor you will always have with
you and you can help them anytime you want' (Mk. 14:7).
However, we do look forward to a time when Jesus comes
again and there will be no more poverty (Rev. 21:1–5).

Suffering injustice

In the meantime, people suffer injustice and meeting their needs through giving them food, shelter and healthcare is not enough. Gary Haugen, President of the International Justice Mission, writes:

> Those who suffer oppression are victimised because they suffer the sins of injustice ... We cannot respond to their need by simply providing them with some material good. To show authentic love to the victim of oppression we must rescue them from their oppressor, bring the perpetrator to account, seek the restoration of the victim and prevent the abuse happening again.[2]

Alfonso Wieland, Director of the Peruvian human rights organisation Peace and Hope, claims:

> Relief or technical support programmes for the poor are good and necessary, but we also need to unmask the social systems in order to transform them. This inevitably implies proposing or reforming laws and working to ensure that the state complies with its function of respecting and upholding human rights for all, especially the weakest.[3]

If we are to care effectively for the poor, we need to tackle the root causes of their poverty by confronting injustice and oppression. If we get involved in confronting poverty, we are inevitably led to tackle injustice, both in individual cases and in systems and structures.

Debt in the Democratic Republic of Congo[4]

The Democratic Republic of Congo (DRC) is rich in natural resources and endowed with vast potential wealth. However, with a GDP per capita of approximately $600, it is one of the poorest countries in the world. More than 80 per cent of the Congolese population are affected by poverty; life expectancy at birth is fifty-one years and the adult literacy rate amounts to 61 per cent. The HIV/AIDS prevalence rate among adults was estimated at 5 per cent in 1999. Much of this poverty and suffering can be traced to economic mismanagement, widespread corruption and political instability.

Mobutu Sese Seko, who ruled DRC (then Zaire) from 1965–97 was one of the world's most corrupt leaders and became one of the world's richest men, hiving off the country's wealth to amass a personal fortune estimated at more than $10 billion, including palaces in Europe and at home. However, the west saw Mobutu as a loyal ally in the Cold War and saw it as politically expedient to continue to support him, even among evidence of such corruption and mismanagement.

In 1978 the IMF appointed one of their staff members, Edwin Blumenthal, to a key post in the Central Bank of Zaire. He resigned two years later, complaining of 'sordid and pernicious corruption' that was so serious that 'there is no chance, I repeat no chance, that Zaire's numerous creditors will ever recover their loans'. Shortly after Blumenthal's report to the IMF, recommending that Zaire receive no more loans, the IMF gave Zaire the largest ever loan given to an African country. In the six years afterwards, the IMF lent Zaire $600 million, the World Bank $650 million and Western governments lent Mobutu nearly $3 billion.

By 1992 banks in Zaire were forced to close because of a lack of funds and inflation reached 16,500 per cent. Economic and political uncertainty continued throughout 1994, with the arrival of approximately one million refugees from Rwanda creating great tension in eastern Zaire. When Blumenthal wrote his report, Zaire's debt was $5 billion and by 1998 (after Mobutu had been overthrown and died), the debt was over $13 billion.

Ordinary people in the country are the ones who suffered during Mobutu's reign and are continuing to suffer while creditors still demand debt repayments. They are suffering due to the corruption in the Zairian government, and the complicity of the International Financial Institutions and the Western Governments who saw their own political interests as more important than the suffering of the Congolese people.

God's Commitment to Justice

In order to be faithful to God's calling, and to bring the full extent of the good news, we therefore need to be involved in tackling injustice.[5] This will usually involve influencing those with power in any given situation.

Although it is hard to provide a meaningful, concise definition, Gary Haugen suggests:

> Fundamentally justice has to do with the exercise of power. To say that God is a God of justice is to say that he is a God who cares about the right exercise of power and authority … so justice occurs when power and authority are exercised in conformity with his standards.[6]

Injustice happens when power is abused and people are prevented from living life to the full as God has intended. Injustice results in poverty, oppression and marginalisation. It prevents people living in harmony with God, with each other and with the creation. It stops people experiencing *shalom*. It happens at all levels:

- *Individual level* – when someone is wrongly imprisoned, a child is sold into prostitution, a woman is in bonded labour or people work full-time in factories and don't earn enough to live on.
- *Community level* – when a community is forcibly removed from its land, denied access to education or discriminated against on grounds of religious beliefs.
- *State level* – when people are denied access to their basic needs of food, shelter, healthcare and a means of production, because the wealth and power are concentrated in

the hands of the few and they misuse their power for their own selfish gain.

- *Global level* – when institutions such as the IMF and World Bank implement policies that have detrimental effect on the poor, or continue to collect debt when money is being taken from healthcare and education.

Most poverty, oppression and suffering can be traced back to unjust acts. Therefore to tackle these issues we need to get to their root causes and tackle the injustices behind them.

Six Reasons Why We Should Tackle Injustice

It is central to God's character

Justice is rooted in the very person of God: 'for I the LORD love justice; I hate robbery and iniquity' (Isa. 61:8). In the Psalms we read that 'the LORD works righteousness and justice for all the oppressed' (Ps. 103:6) and that 'righteousness and justice are the foundation of [God's] throne' (Ps. 89:14). Injustice manifests itself in lives that do not reflect the glory and image of God. As Gary Haugen reminds us:

> In regard to injustice we can trust in four solid truths about his character. God loves justice and, conversely, hates injustice. God has compassion for those who suffer injustice – everywhere around the world, without distinction of favour. God judges and condemns those who perpetrate injustice. God seeks active rescue for the victims of injustice.[7]

It is a command

God's commands and laws are a reflection of his character and a guide to how he wants us to live. In Deuteronomy the

Israelites are commanded to walk in the ways of God because he 'defends the cause of the fatherless and the widow, and loves the alien, giving him food and clothing' (Dt. 10:18). Oppressing the poor shows contempt for God (Prov. 14:31).

There are hundreds of references to God's hatred of injustice and the fact that he brings justice, so there can be no doubt what he thinks and what he requires us to do. One of the clearest examples is in Micah 6:8: 'He has showed you, O man, what is good. And what does the LORD require of you? To act justly and to love mercy and to walk humbly with your God.' This shows that those who are poor in spirit (i.e. walking humbly with God) will be those who also seek justice and have mercy on those who are suffering, and on those who perpetrate the injustice.

Justice and righteousness

Justice and righteousness come from the same family of words in both Greek and Hebrew. This means that justice and righteousness are interchangeable in our Bibles. We are people who have been made righteous by faith and we therefore seek to live a righteous/just life. However, this righteousness/justice is not only part of a private relationship with Jesus, but has social and corporate dimensions. A righteous person will seek justice for others. With this interpretation, those who 'hunger and thirst for righteousness' (Mt. 5:6) are those who also hunger and thirst for justice. Conversely, those who seek justice for others should seek to live righteously themselves. Righteousness has for too long been seen as individual piety and justice as something that is independent of character. Hence, we are told, you cannot judge a leader on their private lives but only on their public actions. As Christians, we are born again and therefore righteousness and justice are both parts of our character as redeemed people. We must resist the tendency to privatise righteousness or confine justice to the public realm.

It relieves poverty and brings freedom

Jesus started his ministry in Capernaum (Lk. 4:18–19) with a reference to the Jubilee year, saying that he had come to bring in a reign that would be characterised by justice. We saw earlier that the Jubilee laws (Lev. 25) have social justice at their core. They were to be enacted so that everyone in Israel would have all that they needed. This involved redistribution of land and money, freeing of slaves and leaving land fallow. This ensured that people knew that their wealth and livelihood was from God, and enabled any injustices to be put right and relationships to be restored. Some of these laws (e.g. leaving the land fallow, cancelling debts) were to be enacted every seven years, and the promised consequences were astonishing:

> There should be no poor among you, for in the land the LORD your God is giving you to possess as your inheritance, he will richly bless you, if only you fully obey the LORD your God and are careful to follow all these commandments I am giving you today (Dt. 15:4–5).

So enacting justice and living in the way that God had planned should result in the eradication of poverty. This was demonstrated in the early church when 'there were no needy persons among them. For from time to time those who owned land or houses sold them, brought the money from the sales, and put it at the apostles feet, and it was distributed to anyone as he had need' (Acts 4:34).

If we truly believe in God's justice, shouldn't we be motivated to take more action?

Actions can free people from their individual cases of oppression or injustice, and bring liberty and hope that they can have a better life in the future (e.g. freeing a child sex-worker who is being held in a brothel and has no way of escaping by herself; defending the case of a prisoner who has been wrongly imprisoned; enabling a girl to go to school who is being kept at home to do domestic chores). In these cases, a change in the wider laws or policies is needed to prevent these situations happening again, but the immediate need is to free these people from their current situations of injustice.

Christians Against Poverty

Christian Against Poverty (CAP) is a national charity in the UK that seeks to help people be free from personal debt and from all of the poverty, worry and relational breakdown that is associated with it. They have debt counsellors throughout the country who are based in local churches. Dan Chapman works as such a counsellor in South London and sees about six people each month. For each new client he visits their home and looks at their financial situation. Together they go through the income and expenses, work out what the client can afford to pay back to the creditors, and draw up a statement of their financial situation. After this Dan contacts the creditors and makes an offer to them of how much the client will pay. The client pays a regular amount to CAP who then pay the creditors on their behalf. This is all completely free of charge and means that CAP is helping the client until they become debt free.

He has recently been able to help a couple with a three-year-old child: 'the mother phoned me up three days before she was due in court to be served an eviction order because she had £4,000 rent arrears. She was suffering depression and stress and felt as though there was no way out. First, we worked out how much of the rent arrears she could afford to pay off each month. Then I contacted the council, with whom I already have a good relationship, and managed to negotiate with them a reasonable repayment schedule. As a result, the family can stay in their house and the mother feels as though her life is back under control. The repayments are manageable so they are able to keep them up.'

On each visit Dan is accompanied by a member of the church, who is there to follow up any other issues with the client, such as links with mothers and toddlers groups, Alpha courses or coun-selling services. In this way there is an ongoing relationship and the church has the opportunity to serve the client in other ways.

It tackles root causes

Tackling social justice can address the root causes of poverty. However, many Christians who are involved in ministries that try and alleviate poverty are focused only on social action or development programmes, not on bringing social justice. Christian development programmes are essential because they work on the ground and enable people to work towards transformed communities that are an expression of the kingdom of God. Even if all injustices were resolved and there were no more policies or laws to change, Christian development would need to continue. This is because it is the practical outworking of men and women living together in restored communities that develops Christian character.

The problem is, social action is usually not enough. Social action and development programmes may bring help to those in need, but they seldom get to the root causes of the problem (e.g. they may alleviate the suffering of those who are unjustly treated, but not tackle the perpetrators of the injustice; they may provide food for those who need it, but not challenge the fact that they do not have land in the first place).

Working for social justice can tackle the root causes of the problem, because it can bring changes in policies and practices of those with power and can even change the balance of power in a given situation (e.g. a change in the law that allows a community to have legal ownership of their land and stay on it; or punishment of police who abuse their power, resulting in a drop in the number of violent incidents). It is primarily about influencing those who have the power to bring about change in any given situation.

To illustrate this point I have included a simple parable, heard from David Gitari, Archbishop of Kenya, showing the practical impacts of going deeper and tackling the causes of poverty, as well as the effects.[8]

There was a factory in which workers were often injured. Seeing these injured workers coming out of the factory a group of Christians decided that they should help them to recover from their injuries. They began by providing antiseptics and bandages. As significant numbers of workers continued to be injured the Christian group redoubled their efforts so that in the end they built a small hospital where the workers could be treated. They also bought an ambulance to bring the injured workers from the factory gates to the hospital. The factory owners contributed generously towards the purchase of the ambulance.

Then one day in all innocence a young girl wondered out loud why so many people were being injured in the factory. This led to a general discussion in the Christian group that eventually led them to ask the factory owners the same question. Finding the owners very evasive in their response, the group investigated further about how factories should be run. They discovered that by law factories should receive regular inspections on health and safety standards. This particular factory had not been inspected for a long time and they suspected it was because a government official was being bribed. The people were therefore being denied their rights under the law due to corrupt practices, and were being injured as a result.

So they mounted a public campaign that eventually led to a government inspection of the factory. The factory owners were forced to introduce many safety features into their production line. This meant that very few workers were injured and the ambulance and hospital were no longer needed for the injured workers from the factory. This campaign managed to tackle the root cause of the problem, not just the effects, and therefore brought lasting change.

It is a sign of the kingdom

The most significant example of God working for justice in the Old Testament is the liberation of his people from oppression in Egypt. This involved physical liberation from slavery, political liberation from an oppressive regime and spiritual liberation so that they could worship God freely. God showed his compassion and desire for justice and freedom:

> The LORD said, 'I have indeed seen the misery of my people in Egypt. I have heard them crying out because of their slave drivers, and I am concerned about their suffering. So I have come down to rescue them from the hand of the Egyptians and to bring them up out of that land into a good and spacious land' (Ex. 3:8–9).

After much persuasion and the performance of signs and wonders, including the ten plagues, Pharaoh freed the Israelites from the physical, economic and spiritual oppression they had been under.

This was a foretaste of the kingdom that Jesus was to bring. Other foretastes are given in Isaiah 65:17–25 and Luke 1:46–55.

Bringing social justice can be a very practical demonstration of the good news that we preach to people. For example, persuading the local school to fulfil its legal responsibility and allow AIDS orphans to attend and receive the same education as everyone else can provide those orphans with evidence of God's love that is being spoken about. Providing legal representation for someone who has been unjustly imprisoned for standing up to the law can help them to see that the good news is wider than just preaching and praying.

It results in blessing for those who do it, and judgement for those who don't

In Isaiah, when God's people are fasting to try and please him, yet oppressing the poor, quarrelling and fighting with each other, he issues a harsh rebuke to them:

> Is this not the kind of fasting I have chosen: to loose the chains of injustice and untie the cords of the yoke, to set the oppressed free and break every yoke? Is it not to share your food with the hungry and to provide the poor wanderer with shelter – when you see the naked, to clothe him, and not to turn away from your own flesh and blood? (Isa. 58:6–7).

If God's people turn and seek justice, he promises that he will guide them always, that they will be a witness to those around and that he will bless them (vv. 9–11).

There are countless other passages that show God's desire for justice, and his judgement when it is neglected. In fact, this was a favourite theme of the Old Testament prophets and neglect of justice usually came hand in hand with neglect of true worship to God:

> You trample on the poor and force them to give you grain. Therefore, though you have built stone mansions, you will not live in them; though you have planted lush vineyards, you will not drink their wine. For I know how many are your offences and how great are your sins. You oppress the righteous and take bribes and you deprive the poor of justice in the courts (Amos 5:11–12).

The Pharisees are also rebuked for neglecting justice: 'Woe to you, teachers of the law and Pharisees, you hypocrites! You give a tenth of your spices – mint, dill and cumin. But

you have neglected the more important matters of the law –
justice, mercy and faithfulness' (Mt. 23:23).

The Role of the Government[9]

When becoming involved with issues of social justice, we
will inevitably come into contact with the government and
other institutions or groups with power. A key aim is to
influence these groups to use their power to bring about the
desired changes in any given situations. For this it is vital to
understand the role of these powers. We start by considering
the role of government as one of the key institutions that
holds and exercises power.

   Government is good and part of God's plan, and not
simply a necessary evil. God created heaven and earth, and
appointed human beings as stewards, to fill the earth and
subdue it and to rule over all living creatures (Gen. 1:28).
However, creation, human beings and government are now
affected by sin. Although government still has a role, it is
both limited and fallen. It is not evil, but corrupted. Romans
13:1–7 and 1 Peter 2:13–17 gives us some guidance into the
role of government.

Judging and punishing evil

The state has a role in judging evil (i.e. rightly identifying it as
evil and punishing it). It exists as 'God's servant, an agent of
wrath to bring punishment on the wrongdoer' but the rulers
'hold no terror for those who do right' (Rom. 13:3–4). However, as God's purpose is always reconciliation and restoration, punishment should hold both love and justice together,
and the aim should be to make things right by administering
justice and restoring things to how they should be. Punishment is not focused on revenge, but on restoration.

Administering justice and protecting the weak

Part of judging and punishing evil is that the state will administer justice and protect weaker members of society from the exploitation by the more powerful. The Psalms speak of God's judgement on unjust rulers and judges, and outline his requirements of them: 'defend the cause of the weak and the fatherless; maintain the rights of the poor and the oppressed. Rescue the weak and the needy; deliver them from the hand of the wicked' (Ps. 82:3–4).

The weaker members of society are often powerless to withstand abuses of economic or political power by other groups and the role of the state is to ensure justice is done and that the poor do not simply become victims of the survival of the fittest. Vaclav Havel, the first president of Czech Republic after the collapse of communism, put his political future on the line and said that the people could judge his government based on how they treated the weakest members of their society.

Promoting human well-being

Government also has the positive task of promoting human well-being. It is there to commend what is right (Rom. 13:3) and 'to do you good' (Rom. 13:4) by establishing the conditions in which the common good can flourish. This biblical idea of well-being is found in *shalom* (material well-being, social justice and peace). This means that the government should promote the necessary conditions whereby every citizen, as well as the church, can flourish. One of the roles of law is therefore to indicate what is right and to discourage wrongdoing. The government also promotes well-being through preserving peace and good order, because if public order is not maintained the very co-existence of people within society is endangered. Paul therefore urges prayers for 'kings and all those in authority so that we may live peaceful and quiet lives in all godliness and holiness. This is good, and pleases God our Saviour, who wants all people to be saved' (1 Tim. 2:1–4).

However, the state is limited, practically, morally and in its essence.

The state is limited practically

The state is powerless to do some things, such as ensure that people truly worship God, or to bring about righteousness. It is therefore limited practically by what it is able to enforce. Paul acknowledges that the law is powerless to change people's hearts or to bring salvation (Rom. 8:3). This refers to Old Testament law but also applies to all types of law. The law can judge evil and even show evil for what it is, but it cannot change people. It can only control outward conduct (Mt. 5).

The state is limited morally

In his governance of the universe, God acknowledges the importance of human freedom, but coupled with responsibility. Human responsibility is dependent on being able to choose between right and wrong. This means governments have a limited role in trying to dictate human behaviour; they should allow for significant freedom and responsibility. Laws should therefore be enacted to bring justice and protect the weak as opposed to trying to dictate all aspects of human behaviour. We should not move the responsibility for trying to influence people's behaviour from the church and family to the state!

The state is limited in essence

Although the state is good, it is also prone to corruption and is based on a different model of power from the one Jesus came to demonstrate (Lk. 22:25; Rev. 13:1–18; 18). The state is affected by individual and institutional sin and can easily become an agent of the kingdom of this world. It therefore has a limited role and is part of the battleground between the forces of the two kingdoms.

The effects of sin mean that individuals use their God-given abilities to exploit others for their own ends, as opposed to serving them. Political structures have often been the means to satisfy the lust for power and glory of certain individuals, and therefore power has been abused for personal gain.

Many of the functions of the state are only necessary in our fallen world (such as judging and punishing evil, including the use of force) and will no longer be needed in the age to come. So, although we know that all powers will be redeemed (Col. 1:15–20), any form of government will look very different in God's kingdom!

So, what are the implications for us as Christians? We each live in a state that should be operating as God intended it, but is fallen and is often far from behaving in a way that honours God, protects the weak, promotes justice and punishes evil. How are we to apply these passages to our modern-day situations?

Being Subject to the State

The most difficult verse in Romans 13 is verse 5: 'it is necessary to submit to authorities'. It has been used for centuries to justify inaction against those in power, even when they have clearly abused their God-given mandate.

The first point to make here is that this passage talks about mutual responsibility, because it also outlines the role of the state ('for he is God's servant to do you good' – v. 4).

Both the government and the citizen have responsibilities. The responsibility of the state is to judge and punish evil, administer justice and protect the weak, and promote human well-being. If the state is fulfilling these roles, our responsibility as citizens is to submit (i.e. to cooperate with the state to enable it to carry on fulfilling these roles).

When Paul wrote Romans, Christians were able to live in relative peace and could obey the state and still be faithful to God's laws. However, there are also examples of authorities turning their back on their mandate to serve, and ruling for their own gain at the expense of others. Revelation 13 and 18 shows 'Babylon the Great', a military and commercial power that has reached the height of arrogant independence from God with the terrible abuse of human beings that follows. The image represents the Roman Empire and reflects John's experience of persecution of the church. It also has broader applications to any power that sets itself up in wilful independence from God's standards. The advice of God is not to respect such an empire as the righteous instrument of God, but to 'Come out of her, my people, so that you will not share in her sins' (Rev. 18: 4).

Therefore, going back to Romans 13, one commentator points out: 'it would be a mistake to understand submission in terms of uncritical obedience ... this leaves us free to dissent, to question the ends for which authority has been put to use.'[10] We have a responsibility to hold authorities to account for how they use their God-given power. This means, among other things, exposing corruption, influencing politicians, ensuring policies are implemented correctly and speaking out against injustice. Significant change could happen if we got involved in this way.

When Paul and Silas were arrested in Philippi (Acts 16), Paul complained that he had been beaten, imprisoned without trial and denied his rights as a Roman citizen. He expected the state to behave in a way that was consistent with its own laws.

When it didn't, he challenged their abuse of power. Peter and John flatly refused to obey the orders of the Jewish ruling council when it commanded them to stop proclaiming that Jesus was the Messiah (Acts 4:18–19; 5:29). They were clear that their primary allegiance was to God.

Jesus rebuked the Pharisees and Sadducees for being too close to the Roman state. His command to 'Give to Caesar what is Caesar's and to God what is God's' (Mk. 12:13–17) was a public rebuke for losing their distinctiveness. Any cooperation with, or allegiance to, the state needs to be secondary to our primary allegiance, which is to God.

Unfortunately, churches have often either been too close to power and have compromised, or opted out and been ineffective. A few days after President Ferdinand Marcos in the Philippines declared martial law, an evangelical leader encouraged people to be thankful because 'now the threat of communism is over and we can preach the gospel unhindered'.[11] Freedom to preach bought at the expense of complicity with injustice was not a victory for the kingdom of God.

Citizenship not only means responsibility towards the government, but also towards other people. Jeremiah told the exiles to seek the welfare of the place in which they were living: 'seek the peace and prosperity of the city to which I have carried you into exile. Pray to the LORD for it, for if it prospers, you too will prosper' (Jer. 29:7). Paul gives advice on what it means to be good citizens: 'do not repay anyone evil for evil. Be careful to do what is right in the eyes of everybody. If it is possible, as far as it depends on you, live at peace with everyone. Do not take revenge, my friends, but leave room for God's wrath' (Rom. 12:17–19). Our responsibility to love our neighbour as ourselves and to be salt and light in the world (Mt. 5:13–16) shows our responsibilities towards our fellow citizens in whatever town and country we live.

Preventing the destruction of livelihoods, Honduras

The Association for a Fairer Society (ASJ) is a social justice organisation working in Honduras. In 1999, the president of Honduras presented a proposal for reform of forestry legislation that would have allowed large sections of national forest to be sold to logging companies who could choose whether or not to reforest the land. The importance of Honduras' national forests for poor farmers and indigenous groups that live in these areas was ignored. Seeing the potentially devastating consequences, ASJ joined with representatives from various sectors (indigenous groups, cooperatives, an evangelical network, agricultural ecologists and farmers groups) to form an alliance called the Honduran Agro-forestry Alliance (AHA) to try to amend the proposed legislation.

AHA hired consultants to analyse the proposal and present reasonable counterproposals to the government. They initiated a media campaign to educate the public about the problem and to pressure the government into negotiating. The media campaign included press conferences, forums on television and radio, press reports, and a web page with detailed analysis and reports. The government agreed that no reform of the forestry legislation would be brought to Congress until a committee consisting of representatives from AHA, as well the government and logging companies had approved it. For eighteen months AHA was involved in negotiations within this committee and continued to use consultants to educate the public, the media and committee members about the counterproposals. Not only were all the proposals of AHA accepted, but also marginal groups such as poor farmers, cooperatives and indigenous groups have been able to participate for the first time in law making that affects them directly.

It is clear, therefore, that there are various options that are not open to us.

One is to align ourselves so closely to the state so that we lose the ability to be distinctive and to hold the state to account. Submission to authorities does not mean subservience to the state. The church always needs to maintain the ability to challenge injustice, tyranny and oppression. It is our God-given mission.

Another is to opt out of the political system altogether as the church would not be able to fulfil its mandate of holding those in authority accountable for their actions. As Edmund Burke said: 'all it takes for evil to succeed is for good men to do nothing'. Practically, it is not possible in most societies to opt out because we live in democracies (where non-participation is effectively a vote for the status quo) and pay taxes, which means we are already part of a state system.

A third option not available is trespassing into the state's area of responsibility, and seeking to run the country. The church and the state have been assigned specific roles by God and it is the responsibility of God's people to ensure that both the church and state stick to these. Earthly power tends to corrupt the church. As the former president of Zambia, Kenneth Kaunda, once said, 'What a nation needs more than anything else is not a Christian ruler in the palace but a Christian prophet within earshot.'

We are called to involvement but to maintain our distinctiveness. If we get involved we can work with God to bring good news to the poor, to challenge injustice and to hold authorities to account to fulfil their God-given role.

Questions for Reflection

- Do you agree that God has a special concern for the poor and those on the edges of society? If so, what implications does this have for the ministry of your church?
- Do you agree that meeting practical needs is not enough and that we need to tackle injustice or the underlying causes of poverty?

- What injustices are you aware of in your local area? In the wider world? What could happen if you got involved? What might happen if you didn't?
- What do you think it means for you to be a good citizen of your country?
- What one action can you take today to start tackling injustices you see around you?

Further Reading

Chester, Tim (ed.), *Justice Mercy and Humility: Integral Mission and the Poor*

Haugen, Gary A., *Good News About Injustice: A Witness of Courage in a Hurting World*

Hughes, Dewi and Matthew Bennett, *God of the Poor*

Maggay, Melba Padilla, *Transforming Society*

Myers, Bryant L., *Walking with the Poor: Principles and Practices of Transformational Development*

Wieland, Alfonso, *In Love With His Justice*

Wink, Walter, *Engaging the Powers: Discernment and Resistance in a World of Domination*

4

Understanding and Engaging
with Power

Introduction

We cannot understand the church's role in social justice
unless we come to terms with the nature of power. In the
previous chapter we looked at one manifestation of power,
the government. This chapter looks at the powers in more
detail – their sources and manifestations and how we
should relate to them.

Understanding Power

Power can be used for good or evil. The state is only one of
the visible faces of power that we see on the Earth. Other
faces include business, international institutions and the
media. In fact, in many instances they have more power
than the state. Therefore, we need to engage with them to
try and bring them more in line with God's original plans.
However, we know that we are engaged in a spiritual battle.
The struggle we are facing is 'against the rulers, against the
authorities, against the powers of this dark world and
against the spiritual forces of evil in the heavenly realms'
(Eph. 6:12). Therefore we need to engage with the powers

at the 'political' level as we see them manifest themselves in the world (e.g. governments passing laws, businesses setting themselves up in a community), as well as engaging at a 'spiritual' level. But first we need to understand the powers.

Powers, as we showed above for the state, are part of God's good creation. Paul tells us that through Christ: 'all things were created; things in heaven and on earth, visible and invisible, whether thrones or powers or rulers or authorities; all things were created by him and for him' (Col. 1:16). The creation narrative in Genesis 1–2 shows us God's intentions with order (seven days), boundaries for the garden, ethical structures (tree of good and evil), limited sovereignty (naming the animals), basic structure of covenant marriage and God's gracious provision in the cherubim to protect Adam and Eve from making their fallen state immortal.

Through the fall, some of these structures, systems, institutions and spiritual beings have fallen and are hostile to God's rule. The earthly powers, systems and structures have been taken over by evil forces (systemic or structural evil) and are operating as if they are self-ordained and are not accountable to God. The book of Revelation gives further insight, showing the many different structures of power working together against God: governments that claim to have the role of God (chapter 13), the influences of pagan culture which take people away from God (chapter 17) and the whole commercial world system which is in direct opposition to God (chapter 18).

So in grappling with the powers we are facing two main sources of evil:

- Structural evil, such as a whole government being run with flagrant disregard for God's laws, and the culture in the government dictating that this will continue.
- Evil beings directly operating against God and against other people (i.e. direct satanic attack).

We also need to take into account our own sinful nature and other people's sinful nature when trying to bring about change (Jer. 17:9). Therefore, if we do not take seriously the spiritual reality behind the manifestations of power, we will only be able to bring about limited change because we won't be tackling the source of the corruption. This is why prayer is such a vital component in tackling any injustice. According to one commentator:

> Paul, in speaking of the 'powers' means more than personal spiritual beings ranged in opposition to the kingdom: he also means depersonalised forces of evil at work in the social climate ('the prince of power of the air') or entrenched in structures of the created order, which have become 'principalities' or realms of the demonic. The sense that we are up against overwhelming forces of institutionalised injustice is founded on the reality that evil has macrocosmic dimensions. Sin expresses itself not only in personal and individual badness such as adultery or perverted sex, but also in corporate and systemic forms such as apartheid in the old South Africa or economic exploitation in many parts of the Third World by native ruling classes and multinational entities.[1]

However, we can take courage that Jesus has the supreme authority and final victory over all of these powers. He casts out demons (Lk. 11:20), destroys the power of Satan (Mk. 3:23–6) and rules over every power (Col. 2:10). Christ's death on the cross was a victory not only over the sin of humankind but over the powers as well. These powers are bound, although they still rule the kingdom of this world for the time being (1 Cor. 15:24–27). One commentator writes of the work on the cross:

> It was no less than the wresting of the entire world order from the strongholds of evil. 'Now is the judgement of the world,

now shall the ruler of this world be cast out …' (Jn. 12:31).
Quite strangely, this overthrowing of the 'prince of the power
of the air' did not happen by the use of force … but by the
nailing of the Son of God on a cross, a shedding of blood that
mysteriously effected forgiveness and the disarming of princi-
palities and powers (Heb. 9:22; Col. 2:13–15).[2]

Although the cross is where Jesus has won the final victory,
the battle is still being played out and that is why we see so
much injustice in the world. Therefore, in becoming
involved in tackling injustice, we become part of that battle
and involve ourselves in confronting evil systems, structures
and beings. The author quoted above goes on to say 'we
must understand that in standing against evil and its social
and structural expressions we are putting ourselves at the
centre of demonic opposition'.[3]

Understanding the nature of power is one thing, but how
do we actually engage with the powers?

Engaging with the Powers

First and foremost we need to keep our eyes firmly fixed
on Jesus and his ultimate victory if we are not to be overwhelmed by the rulers of this world. We are given God's
power to engage in this battle:

> Therefore put on the full armour of God, so that when the day
> of evil comes, you may be able to stand your ground, and after
> you have done everything, to stand. Stand firm then, with the
> belt of truth buckled round your waist, with the breastplate of
> righteousness in place, and with your feet fitted with the readi-
> ness that comes from the gospel of peace. In addition to all this,
> take up the shield of faith, with which you can extinguish all
> the flaming arrows of the evil one. Take the helmet of salvation

and the sword of the spirit. Which is the word of God. And pray in the spirit on all occasions with all kinds of prayers and requests. With this in mind, be alert and always keep on praying for all the saints (Eph. 6:13–18).

According to one author, 'we cannot wrestle with the powers faithfully without a vision of the final pacification of the powers when Christ comes again and establishes the new heaven and the new earth'.[4] We need to keep an eternal perspective on our current struggles. We need to see the world as God sees it.

In the past, different Christian groups have tried to engage with the powers in different ways, depending on how they have understood the powers and which sources and manifestations of the powers they have seen as most important. Four historic approaches to the powers can be represented as follows:[5]

Approach	Exorcism and intercession	Suffering and powerlessness	Creative participation	Just revolution
View of power	Demonic influence on people (ignores structures)	Evil forces have taken over structures (so they are now inherently bad)	Structures are fallen (but can be redeemed)	Structures are oppressive (but no spiritual view of power)
Means to deal with power	Prayer – exorcism and intercession	Identify with suffering, model powerlessness, model an alternative, speak out prophetically	Work for policy change, stand for election, hold politicians to account, address individual cases	Civil disobedience, symbolic actions

Aim in dealing with power	Spiritual liberation of people	To witness to fallenness and shame powers into change	Participation in redemption of structures – social change	Social change
Denominations	Charismatic	Anabaptist	Mainline	Liberation theology

In reality, any approach may be useful and in a given situation it is likely that more than one approach would be used, as has been shown in chapters 7–12. Some shorter examples, where action has been focused mainly on one approach, are given below. They do not cover all approaches (e.g. they miss out working for policy change and standing for election), because these are covered in detail in the other chapters elsewhere in the book.

Prayer (see also chapters on Kenya and Rwanda)

In their book about ministry in a housing estate in the outskirts of Birmingham, UK, Wallace and Mary Brown show the power of prayer in defeating a gang that was terrorising the neighbourhood:

> At the window I saw the usual scene. Gang members were lolling around the walls, shouting and swearing. A bottle crashed to the ground and shattered on our front path. Others were intent on the notice board, ripping off the latest offering and defacing the painted sign with a knife. In the morning I knew I would find discarded contraceptives. My heart fluttered as I considered, once again, what to do.[6]

They were praying and God gave Mary a vision, based on the prophet Nehemiah, when he placed guards on the walls of the temple as he was rebuilding it. They were to ask God to place guardian angels on the walls around their church and fight this battle on the spiritual level:

> Feeling slightly foolish, I asked God to place guardian angels all round the walls, to make them safe, and to bring godliness to our lawns and boundaries ... The effect was immediate and astonishing. Within a few days the gang started to break up. From the thirty-five swearing, screaming youths of the previous week, the number dropped to about ten and then by the following week a mere two or three. Mary and I continued to go out and pray day-by-day: 'LORD, keep your guardian angels around these walls, please.' And so he did. The relief was absolute. After year upon year of human failure, the terrible 'siege' of the church and vicarage was broken by the supernatural presence of God's angels. People started to come in unhindered. My family unexpectedly tasted freedom, and it was wonderful. Mary was able to walk out of the house and I could relax. What's more, the mob did not move to pastures new – they totally broke up![7]

Modelling powerlessness

This often involves symbolic actions of defiance against those in power, or actions that are means to shame powers into changing their behaviour. Often the actions are done when people think that there are no alternatives (e.g. that the government is so bad that there is no other way of trying to engage it, the only option is to witness to them from afar).

Henry Olonga, the Zimbabwean cricketer, made such a stand at the cricket world cup in Zimbabwe in early 2003. He and team mate Andy Flower wore black armbands to protest against the death of democracy in his country under President Robert Mugabe. In a country where dissenters are subject to violence and intimidation, this was a bold gesture, but Olonga was resolute in his stand: 'I have thought about the costs of making a stand and I think Christianity

transcends everything else. Christians are called to speak out
against evil, to speak out against things that are wrong and that are
wicked. In the face of wickedness, my stand is simply that I am
merely doing my duty as a Christian.'[8]

Olonga was left out of the final match and soon afterwards
announced his retirement from international cricket. He said, 'the
stand I took earlier in the World Cup has undoubtedly had repercussions that have affected both my career and my personal life. I
was never under the illusion that my stand would have no consequences but I believe that one should have the courage of one's
convictions in life and do all one can to uphold them. I believe that if I
were to continue to play for Zimbabwe in the midst of the prevailing
crisis I would do so only by neglecting the voice of my conscience.'[9]

Individual cases of injustice
(see also chapters on Peru, Cambodia and Kenya)

Policy change may only provide a medium- or long-term
solution, yet individuals who are suffering injustices need
immediate help to free them from their situations. This
could involve representing their cases in court if they have
been wrongly imprisoned, working with local police
authorities to motivate raids on brothels to rescue the
young girls held in forced prostitution and arrest the perpetrators, including the brothel owners, who are holding them
in sexual slavery, and freeing a woman held under bonded
labour. US-based advocacy organisation International
Justice Mission (IJM) has been involved in a number of
cases like this, one of which is outlined here:[10]

Joyti is a 14-year-old girl from a rural town in India who was abduc-
ted and drugged by four women who sold her to a brothel in
Bombay. She was locked away in an underground cell and severely
beaten with metal rods, plastic pipe and electrical cords until sub-
mitting to provide sex to the customers. She had to work seven

days a week, servicing twenty to forty customers a day. IJM arranged for criminal investigators to infiltrate the brothel where Joyti was being held. Video surveillance technology was used to document the evidence of where she was being held and who was running the brothel. Secure police contacts were mobilised to raid the brothel and release Joyti. She was referred to a place of residential Christian aftercare where she is now being looked after. Her brothel keeper was arrested and is facing prosecution. She has been freed from her situation and can now attempt to build up a life again.

Civil disobedience

This occurs when people deliberately disobey rules or laws of the government or other institutions, as a way of trying to bring about change or showing dissatisfaction with the current situation. It usually happens when people think the laws are immoral and they have tried all other forms of legal protest, but without success, and civil disobedience is only considered if there is no other option.

Civil disobedience is often an issue that causes difficulties for Christians, with people asking 'how far can you go?' Some are put off any involvement in issues of social injustice even before they have started to get involved. Fuller treatment of this issue is given in chapter 16 where violence is dismissed as an option open to Christians and civil disobedience is seen as a last resort.

In the boycott of the buses in America, Martin Luther King and the boycotters provide an example of civil disobedience that was non-violent and effective (see chapter 6). They boycotted the buses and continued to do so after a law was passed saying that these actions were illegal. However, King always emphasised the non-violent nature of the protests: 'the non-violent resister must often express his protest through non-cooperation or boycotts, but non-cooperation and boycotts are not ends in themselves; they are merely means to awaken a sense of moral shame in the opponent. The end is redemption and reconciliation.'¹¹ Within a year segregation of the buses had ended.

Symbolic actions

These are often closely associated with civil disobedience or with identifying with those who are suffering. Symbolic actions aim to highlight specific injustices. They may include actions such as sending back a product to a supermarket if they are treating their workers badly, a silent vigil for those who have 'disappeared', staging a media stunt outside an arms fair, tearing up call-up papers for the Vietnam war or non-payment of a tax. Symbolic actions can be a powerful and important part of campaigning.

Exposing corruption and injustice
(see also chapters on Kenya, Peru and Rwanda)

One of the ways that injustice is allowed to continue is that it is often hidden and the perpetrators know they will get away with it. However, if unjust actions are exposed for what they are, then this is likely to bring people to justice and to stop those actions being repeated in the future.

St John's Community Centre works with the slum dwellers of Pumwani, Kenya. For a long time the community has been prone to police harassment and brutality, including beatings, illegal detention and extortion of money. The community had confidence in neither the law enforcers nor themselves to be able to do anything about the situation. In 2000, Pumwani Arts Academy, a group involved in educating the people on human rights, started to work with St John's Community Centre and the community to address the issues. They informed the local police that they were going to have shows and invited them to attend. The performances involved a play and dances, informing the community about their rights and encouraging them to challenge any form of police harassment.

Unknown to the group, plain-clothed policemen were present. They took careful notes and reported what was going on to their senior officers. Immediately afterwards the police brutality and harassment reduced drastically and the community is now safer. The police knew that the community were aware of their rights and equipped to challenge any injustices – they knew they would get caught! Things were out in the open.

Initially, many people were afraid that the play would make the relationship between the police and the community worse. However, due to the transparent way it was done, and the involvement of the whole community, relationships have in fact improved.

Working Under Oppressive Governments

Many Christians live in countries without a democratic government and where the church is persecuted. This persecution can range from imprisonment under false accusations (Peru), discrimination in finding jobs (India), no freedom to meet together (Sudan) to threats of death for becoming a Christian or for telling others about Christ (Afghanistan). In the face of such persecution, what options are open to Christians to engage with the powers?

As each situation is so different, we do not attempt to offer a blueprint for involvement, or even to offer detailed guidelines. On the previous pages we have shown various possible ways of engaging with the powers. In a healthy democracy it is likely that Christians would use all of these methods over time. However, under persecution, the options are likely to be more limited. In some situations any political activity could be extremely dangerous and even life threatening for those involved. You cannot avoid all danger, but you can do a great deal to minimise the risks and

make sure that everyone is aware of the possible consequences of any activity. A few ways to do this are:

- Talk about the possible consequences with all those
  likely to be affected. Ensure they are both happy with any
  activity taking place and aware of what could happen.
- Pray at all times for God's intervention and protection
  and seek God's will for your actions.
- Build good contacts with other groups who may be persecuted in the same way, and with groups in the country who
  may be able to help (e.g. human rights lawyers). Build
  good contacts with 'insiders' in the government or ruling
  authority who may be able to exert pressure on others if
  something happens to threaten your security. Build good
  relationships with organisations outside of the country
  that may be able to help you in times of need (e.g. Amnesty
  International, International Justice Mission).
- Remember that you are operating as one part of the global
  church. Seek help from other parts of the church. Work
  with other parts so that each part can play to their strengths.
- Build your legitimacy with the government, so that it is
  clear that the church plays an important role in society
  (whether in caring for those in need, providing education,
  undertaking development work, etc.).
- Always act in love and with integrity and avoid any
  deliberately inflammatory statements or actions that you
  know will get you into trouble.

Conclusion

There are various ways of engaging with power. We are
called to get involved when we see injustice perpetrated or
power being abused. Using a range of methods including
prayer, political involvement, speaking out and identifying

with those who are suffering will increase our chances of being effective. In doing so we can work with God to make his good news a reality to those who are suffering. What could happen if you got involved?

Questions for Reflection

- What are the different options open to tackling injustice for the church or individual Christians in your country?
- Has your church tended to favour one of the approaches outlined in the table to the detriment of the others? If so, what may you need to do to rectify this situation?
- Would you ever consider breaking the law (civil disobedience)? Under what circumstances?
- If you are living in a country where the church is persecuted, what options do you think are open to you to tackle injustice?

Further Reading

Carson, Clayborne (ed.), *The Autobiography of Martin Luther King Jr.*

Haugen, Gary A., *Good News About Injustice: A Witness of Courage in a Hurting World*

Hughes, Dewi and Matthew Bennett, *God of the Poor*

Maggay, Melba Padilla, *Transforming Society*

Wallis, Jim, *The Soul of Politics: A Practical and Prophetic Vision for Change*

Wieland, Alfonso, *In Love With His Justice*

Wink, Walter, *Engaging the Powers: Discernment and Resistance in a World of Domination*

5

Jesus' Approach to Power and Politics

Jesus engaged with the Jewish political structures of his day and it was his political actions that were ultimately responsible for his death. He challenged those in authority by words and actions, spoke out against injustice and worked with those on the edges of society. However, he didn't conform to the stereotypes of those in power. He modelled servant leadership, he worked with 'nobodies' to achieve his plans, he did not use force and he taught and demonstrated love for his enemies. This was kingdom politics. It was to be played by new rules. It was not focused on short-term gain but had an eternal perspective.

Prophet, Priest and King

Before giving some examples of how Jesus engaged with power and politics, it is worth looking back to the roles of leaders in Israel to understand what roles the Messiah was expected to fulfil. In the Old Testament there were three roles for the leaders of God's people, namely prophets, priests and kings.[1]

The prophets declared God's will and character. They told things about the future (Isa. 7:14, Jer. 31:3) and also revealed God's purpose to people in concrete situations, usually concerning judgement over idolatry and oppression, and the need for repentance and faith (Amos 2:6–8). Prophets also kept a spiritual and moral barometer of Israel (Hos. 9:8) and were ministers of hope, proclaiming the ultimate rule of God. Their role was to tell people what was wrong and why, and how they needed to change.

The priests had several functions, but they were chiefly the mediators between God's people and God himself. They were teachers of God's law (Dt. 27:9); the ones who could intercede on behalf of the people and make atonement for sin (Lev. 9; 16); they maintained the sanctuary and the sacrificial system (Num. 18:1), and they discerned the will of God (Ex. 28:30).

The kings were anointed representatives to bring order, justice and peace to the nation. They had responsibility to 'defend the cause of the weak and the fatherless and maintain the rights of the poor and oppressed' (Ps. 82:3). They were the agents of God's rule on earth, subservient to him and put in place to do his will and ensure that his people also did his will.

According to Stevens:

> Israel needed all three … all three pointed beyond themselves towards the eternal purposes of God for Israel. But they did more. They equipped Israel to accomplish God's purposes of being a 'kingdom of priests and a holy nation' (Ex. 19:6) and so fulfil God's promise to Abraham to bless all nations. Not only Israel but also the world needed all three.[2]

Jesus embodied prophet (Isa. 61:1–2), priest (Heb. 7:11–28) and king (Ps. 89:35–37). He spoke, demonstrated, lived and applied the word of God; he mediated between God and man and taught God's law; and he demonstrated justice and peace as the hallmark of his new kingdom. Maggay notes:

The church as prophet, priest and king requires the gifts and resources of the whole body of Christ. Speaking the Word in places of injustice and suffering needs gifts of communicative power. Bringing a world of need to God calls for men and women who will take time to listen to God and the heart-cry of a turbulent world. Managing a bruised creation exacts costly servanthood from those whose skills and training normally go to the highest bidder in the market place or are exported to countries of affluence.[3]

It is not easy or necessarily useful to split each of his actions below into prophetic, priestly or kingly roles, because Jesus had an integrated ministry and embodied all roles in his person. But it is useful to bear in mind that these actions were part of Jesus' ministry to be the true prophet, priest and king and, following in his footsteps, we as the church are called to speak out prophetically, to intercede for others and to work with God in establishing his kingdom. Looking to Jesus as our role model is essential to give us guidance for effective ministry.

Jesus the New Politician

Jesus was not a 'politician' in the sense that he held a political office or sought political power in the Roman state. He did neither. However, this is only a tiny part of political action and it would be naive to argue for an apolitical church from these facts. This is because Jesus was political. He engaged with power, he got involved in decisions that affected the people, he sought justice and his actions brought him into direct confrontation with those in authority, both religious and political leaders. His political activity of challenging the power of Pontius Pilate, Caesar, the Pharisees, teachers of the law and Sadducees took him to the cross. Those who felt threatened, who wanted to maintain the status quo, crucified him.

He challenged corruption, hypocrisy and injustice in Jewish society

Jesus was not afraid of the Jewish authorities and his words and actions challenged them and the behaviour they encouraged. When entering the Temple in Jerusalem, the seat of Jewish religious power, he

> began driving out those who were buying and selling there. He overturned the tables of the money-changers and the benches of those selling doves ... and as he taught them he said, 'Is it not written: "My house will be called a house of prayer for all nations?" But you have made it a "den of robbers"' (Mk 11:15–17).

He was attacking the corrupt practices of money changing that caused the poor to suffer most. He could not stand the hypocrisy of the ruling Jewish powers and the way their teaching misled the people. He warned his disciples to 'be on your guard against the yeast [teaching] of the Sadducees and Pharisees' (Mt. 16:6).

Perhaps one of the harshest criticisms of the Pharisees is found in Luke 11 when Jesus speaks out against them: 'woe to you Pharisees because you ... neglect justice and the love of God ... love the most important seats in the synagogues ... are like unmarked graves which people walk over without knowing it ... load people down with burdens they can hardly carry ... build tombs for the prophets, and it was your ancestors who killed them ... have taken away the key to knowledge' (Lk. 42–52). Jesus condemns their disregard for justice, their use of power for gain, and their leading people astray. These prophetic actions of Jesus were profoundly political because they threatened the privileged positions of the Pharisees, Sadducees and teachers of the law, undermined the respect the people had for them and ultimately drove the religious authorities to plot his death (Lk. 20:19).

He associated with those on the edges of society

Jesus went out of his way to accept everyone he met and to associate with those who were on the edges of society. He started his ministry in Galilee, away from the social, political and religious centre of Jerusalem. He was accused by the Pharisees of associating with 'tax collectors and sinners' – an act that was considered to pollute the character of the one who did it. He accepted the anointing by a 'sinful woman' (Lk. 7:36–50) and said that God accepted her for her faith and her love. He outlined his mission as being specifically for 'sinners': 'it is not the healthy who need a doctor, but the sick. I have not come to call the righteous, but sinners to repentance' (Lk. 5:31).

When the disciples stopped people bringing children to Jesus, he rebuked them: 'let the little children come to me' (Lk. 18:16). He also healed the blind, the sick, those who were possessed by demons and those whom no one else would speak to, such as the woman who had been bleeding for twelve years and the man who was chained outside the city. Even in his death, he spoke with love and compassion to one of the men who were crucified with him (Lk. 23:43). This was visible evidence of the good news to the poor that he came to bring (Lk. 4:18–19) and through these actions he was fulfilling God's law, summed up in the commandment 'love your neighbour as yourself'.

He challenged the Jewish leaders because he was identifying with those in need, those that had been neglected by society. He was giving them the pride of place in his ministry, not the religious authorities that had expected to be treated with deference and respect. Jesus knew that his main allegiance was to God and this meant identifying with the poor and showing the Jewish society up for its neglect. The church needs to continue this preferential option for those on the edges of society.

He used 'nobodies' to bring about his kingdom

Jesus' disciples were largely uneducated and were from Galilee, considered a backwater in Israel. It would have been expected that any leader would start their mission in Jerusalem, but by starting in Galilee Jesus is forcing the powerful to look to the powerless for wisdom, for leadership and for guidance. This was a challenge to the arrogance and self-importance of the whole system, and showed the Jewish leaders that they were not irreplaceable. In fact, they were more of a problem than a means for God to bring about his kingdom.

Jesus uses ordinary people, who humbly submit to him, to bring about his kingdom. As Paul says to the Christians in Corinth:

> Think of what you were when you were called. Not many of you were wise by human standards; not many were influential; not many were of noble birth. But God chose the foolish things of the world to shame the wise; God chose the weak things of the world to shame the strong. He chose the lowly things of this world and the despised things – and the things that are not – to nullify the things that are, so that no one may boast before him (1 Cor. 1:27–29).

By using those who were seen as dispensable by society, Jesus challenged the way power was seen and used, and challenged the values upon which society was based. He was also demonstrating the alternative kingdom that he was bringing to birth. As the church we are called to do the same.

He mediated between God and man

Jesus prayed frequently for his followers and for the world (Jn. 17:6–26), mediating between God and people. We are also told that 'if anyone does sin, we have one who speaks to the Father in our defence – Jesus Christ, the Righteous One' (1 Jn. 1:2). Jesus plays the priestly role of interceding (Rom. 8:34) and this role of intercession is vital for the church to continue, in the confidence that Jesus is interceding there with us.

He modelled servant leadership

Jesus started his life in a stable in Bethlehem. Throughout his earthly ministry, he did not lord it over others but stressed the fact that he had come to serve. He identified himself (Mt. 8:17) with the suffering servant of Isaiah 53: 'He was despised and rejected by men, a man of sorrows, and familiar with suffering. Like one from whom men hide their faces, he was despised, and we esteemed him not.' When James and John asked Jesus if one could sit on his right and the other on his left in his kingdom (Mk. 10:37), Jesus restated why he had come (v. 45): 'For even the Son of Man did not come to be served, but to serve, and to give his life as a ransom for many.' He also says that this is the path for those who are following him (v. 42): 'You know that those who are regarded as rulers of the Gentiles lord it over them, and their high officials exercise authority over them. Not so with you. Instead, whoever wants to be great among you must be your servant, and whoever wants to be first must be slave of all.'

God's kingdom is characterised by service and humility. He demonstrated his servant nature by washing his disciples' feet, and challenged them: 'Now that I, your LORD and Teacher, have washed your feet, you should also wash one another's feet. I have set you an example that you should do as I have done for you' (Jn. 13:14–15). However, Jesus also demanded absolute loyalty so servant leadership does not preclude the exercise of authority, but focuses on how it is used.

He gave up his power, but defeated all powers

Jesus, who is God, became man. He 'made himself nothing, taking the very nature of a servant, being made in human likeness. And being found in appearance as a man, he humbled himself and became obedient to death – even death on a cross' (Phil. 2:7–8). He wilfully gave up the power he had and became powerless. But the result was that the ultimate power, death 'has been swallowed up in victory. "Where O death is your victory? Where O death is your sting?"' (1 Cor. 15:54–55). In his death on the cross Jesus confronted the powers of the universe and defeated them. There is no power that Jesus has not subdued to his will or is outside his redemptive purposes (Col. 2:15). Therefore, when we engage with power, we need to remember who is already victorious, but we also need to remember that we are engaging 'against the rulers, against the authorities, against the powers of this dark world and against the spiritual forces of evil in the heavenly realms' (Eph. 6:12). Tackling injustice is therefore a spiritual as well as a political battle.

His ultimate allegiance was not to the Emperor, but to God

In his teaching about Roman authority, Jesus made it clear that he obeyed the law of the land where this did not conflict with God's law. When questioned about taxes he concluded by saying, 'Give to Caesar what is Caesar's and to God what is God's'(Mk. 12:13–17). He is thus acknowledging a legitimate role for the state and encouraging Jews to be model citizens in obeying the state. However, the main emphasis of this instruction in Mark's Gospel was to 'give to God what is God's'. Jesus said this just after he had overturned the tables in the temple and rebuked the Jews for making the temple into a 'den of robbers'. He makes it clear that his primary allegiance is to God the Father. In the garden of Gethsemane Jesus prays, 'Abba, Father. Everything is possible for you. Take this cup from me. Yet not what I will, but what you will' (Mk. 14:36).

He did not use force to gain what he wanted

He rode into Jerusalem on a donkey as a sign of humility, identifying with the king in the book of Zechariah and stressing his peaceful aims: 'See, your king comes to you, righteous and having salvation, gentle and riding on a donkey, on a colt, the foal of a donkey' (Mt. 21:5; cf. Zech. 9:9). Jesus rebuked one of his followers for lashing out with his sword during his arrest (Lk. 22:51) and challenges his attackers, 'am I leading a rebellion, that you have come with swords and clubs?' (v. 52). When called before Pilate to answer his accusation of being the King of the Jews, Jesus has a very different kingship in mind: 'my kingdom is not of this world. If it were, my servants would fight to prevent my arrest by the Jews. But now my kingdom is from another place' (Jn. 18:36). His kingdom was to come about by speaking the truth and not by force.

He trained others to carry on his work

Jesus did not focus all power on himself, but trained others to carry on his work. He spent three years with twelve disciples, explaining things to them that he did not explain to others (Lk. 8:10) and giving them unique insights into his mission. Within this twelve he chose three to have even more personal training (Peter, James and John). He also used other disciples and sent out the seventy-two to do his work. He trusted those who were following him and allowed them to learn through getting involved (Lk. 9:1–9). At the same time, he made it very clear what the cost of following in his footsteps would be: 'those who do not take up their cross and follow me are not worthy of me. Those who find their life will lose it, and those who lose their life for my sake will find it' (Mt. 10:38–39). When involved in development work or in tackling injustice we need to remember Jesus' example of including others. He encouraged people to get involved from the start, allowed them to make mistakes and supported their growth. He did not try and do everything himself.

He taught love for enemies

When Jesus was in Israel, the Jewish people loathed the Romans who had ended their earlier freedom and were now their occupying force. They spoke against them, some of the Zealots killed Roman soldiers, and nearly all people were expecting a Messiah to come and re-establish an earthly kingdom for the Jewish people. However, Jesus taught love for enemies instead of hate, something which would have shocked all but the most faithful of Jews. He taught his followers to 'Love your enemies and pray for those who persecute you' (Mt. 5:44), and said that 'Blessed are the merciful, for they will be shown mercy' (Mt. 5:7). The most profound example of love and forgiveness was on the cross when Jesus cried out: 'Father, forgive them, for they do not know what they are doing' (Lk. 23:34). Jesus taught love as the centre of all that he did, which included a love for enemies and those on the margins of society. This was a dramatic way to challenge the very basis of power in his day. When tackling injustice or oppression it is easy to turn anger at the situation into hatred for the perpetrators. Jesus' call to love our enemies is a challenging reminder to love both those who suffer injustice and those who perpetrate it.

Conclusion

When considering how we approach power, we should first go to Jesus' example. He was driven by love and had reconciliation at the heart of his message – reconciliation to God and to others. He preached and demonstrated service and the deep desire for righteousness and justice. He told his disciples to obey the earthly authorities but that their primary allegiance was to God. However, he was not afraid to challenge all authority when it was unjust and disobedient to God. In fact, he challenged hypocrisy and corruption at all levels of society. He associated with those on the margins and worked with ordinary people to bring about his kingdom, training them for ministry and supporting them as they made mistakes. This is the example we are called to as Christians, as we seek to follow the political example of Jesus. He is a role model every bit as relevant today as he was 2000 years ago.

Questions for Reflection

- How would you answer those who say that Jesus was not political?
- How does Jesus' approach to power differ from those in power today?
- How well do you follow Jesus' approach to power? What do you need to change?

- How well does the church follow Jesus' approach to power? What does it need to change?

Further Reading

Kraybill, Donald B., *The Upside-down Kingdom*

Stevens, R. Paul, *The Abolition of the Laity: Vocation, Work and Ministry in a Biblical Perspective*

Wink, Walter, *Engaging the Powers: Discernment and Resistance in a World of Domination*

Yoder, John Howard, *The Politics of Jesus*

6

The Christian Heritage of Political Involvement

Introduction

This chapter outlines a history of the involvement of God's people with the state or governing authority. To church historians this chapter is bound to be tantalisingly brief. It merely scratches the surface of many of the main events and movements that have shaped Christian political thought and action in almost 2000 years of history. To those who have only a sketchy knowledge of their Christian heritage of involvement in social and political issues, I hope it will whet your appetite to delve further into this topic.[1]

Political involvement is not a new issue for the church in the twentieth and twenty-first centuries. If we use a definition of political involvement that includes all engagement with authorities and those in power, then Christians have been involved politically for nearly 2000 years. Most of the involvement has been determined by the church's view of the role of the state and the role of church in society, which has also been influenced by the social and political contexts of different times. When this has been based on a wrong or incomplete understanding it has often been dangerous or meant the church has been ineffective in its role of salt and light in society. This again underlies the importance of having a correct biblical theology of the kingdom of God, the mission of the church, and the role of the state and of power.

The Early Church

The first three centuries

In the early centuries of the Christian era, Christians lived as supportive communities, sharing everything they had (Acts 2:42–47). By the end of the first century they were despised and misunderstood by the majority and suffered sporadic persecution. The Bible does not record them having much contact with the state or other powers, except to argue that they would continue to speak about God (Acts 4:18–19, 5:29) and to pray for the rulers (1 Tim. 2:1–4). They asserted their supreme allegiance to God, not to the state, although they were happy to obey laws if they did not contravene God's laws. The spirit of that age is captured in the second century AD *Letter to Diognetus*, which explains how Christians lived:

> They dwell in their own countries, but only as sojourners; they bear their share in all things as citizens, and they endure all hardships as strangers. Every foreign country is a fatherland to them, and every fatherland is foreign ... Their existence is on earth, but their citizenship is in heaven. They obey the established laws, and they surpass the laws in their own lives. They love all men, and they are persecuted by all ... In a word, what the soul is in a body, thus the Christians are in the world.

The author of the *Letter to Diognetus* is classed with a group of second-century writers called the Apologists. They argued with the authorities for the rights of Christians to live without persecution in the Roman Empire. Their key argument was that Christians were not subversive. Rather, Christians' lives displayed the sort of goodness that any state needs in order to flourish. The Roman Empire was tolerant of a diversity of religions and the Apologists argued that Christians should be included because they were not a threat to the integrity of the state. Due to the climate of persecution it would have been unwise for the Christians to try and engage directly in the state political system. However, it is still clear that they had significant impact by living as exemplary citizens wherever they were. There have been many occasions since the early centuries when Christians have used the same arguments with repressive regimes.

Development of the Christian state

The conversion of the Emperor Constantine in AD 312 led to the adoption of Christianity as the favoured religion of the Roman Empire. In AD 380, during the reign of Theodosius, it was adopted as the official state religion. Temples were destroyed and turned into churches, heretics and non-Christians were persecuted and all non-Christian practices and customs were prohibited – although the laws were not rigidly enforced. After three centuries of persecution, most Christians readily welcomed this new situation. Many saw the Roman Empire as God's intended instrument for the establishment of Christianity in the world, with the church called upon to mould its public life and institutions. Constantine united the east and west of the Roman Empire in AD 324 and in the east (present-day Turkey) he built a new Rome, Constantinople (now Istanbul), from where he ruled the empire.

Greek-speaking leaders dominated the church in this new capital and this heightened tensions between the Greek-dominated Eastern Church and the Latin-speaking Christians of the west who were centred in Rome. This sowed the seeds for the division of the church into east and west, Orthodox and Catholic. This split has dominated church history since the tenth century, when the tensions resulted in an acrimonious parting of the ways.

This model of church–state relations, which has long dominated the west, has proved a mixed blessing. It resulted in religious freedom for Christians, persecution fell dramatically and many pagan practices stopped. There were also many more humane laws introduced. However, heretics and non-Christians were persecuted. The Emperor became the supreme governor of the church and could intervene in its affairs and the state apparatus was used to promote Christianity through coercion. As the church apparatus became essential to the state, those in authority began to exert influence and control over church appointments. The increased status of these church appointments also began to attract people for the wrong reasons. The result was an increasing number of 'worldly' bishops who were focused more on prestige and power than on the health of the church as a counterbalance to abuse of political power. The church also tended to place too much emphasis on the role of the state in bringing about change in society, thereby abdicating its own responsibility.

In the east, the model of a very close relationship between the state and the church was consolidated. This became the standard approach in all the countries that came to be dominated by Greek Orthodoxy. This is why, even after a long period of repression under communism, Orthodoxy is trying hard to re-establish a privileged relationship with the state in countries like Romania and Russia. It is also pushing hard for legislation that will curtail the freedom of other Christian denominations. In Eritrea, the Greek Orthodox Church, which has worked closely with the socialist government, has recently managed to close down the evangelical Kale Heywet churches.

Separation of church and state

When the Visigoths sacked Rome in AD 410, Augustine, the Bishop of Hippo (which was situated in present-day Algeria), set out to defend the accusation that the Roman Empire had collapsed due to the acceptance and promotion of Christianity. He did this by showing that good Christians were also called to be good citizens. This became the first part of his highly influential book, *The City of God*. However, it soon became apparent 'that the crucial question was not whether civil society could survive Christianity but whether Christianity itself could survive its integration into civil society'.[2] In other words, could Christianity survive as the state religion, or would it inevitably be compromised to unacceptable levels?

Augustine challenged the view that the state was the chosen instrument for the establishment of Christianity. The rest of *The City of God* concerns itself with a history of human society in terms of two cities, the city of God and the earthly city.

Augustine believed 'that the level of justice of which societies [were] capable [was] always considerably lower than that to which individuals [could] aspire'[3] and a state could never live up to the ethical demands of the gospel. His views were influenced by the blatant injustices he saw perpetrated by the Roman state and the persecutions that Christians had previously suffered. Therefore, an earthly empire had a very limited function to minimise disorder and maintain peace, as opposed to achieving the right order or promoting the welfare of its citizens. Augustine asked:

> Concerning this life of mortals, which is lived and ended in a few days, what difference does it make whose governance a man who is about to die lives under, so long as those who rule do not compel him to impiety and sin?[4]

He believed that the main concern of Christians, as citizens of the city of God, was to worship the true God. They should only participate in activities of the earthly city that are necessary for the maintenance of peace, and only become concerned if laws present a hindrance to their worship and practice, and spread of the gospel. Augustine maintained that there is some overlap between the two cities but, because he had a very low opinion of the state option, he saw any 'political' activity as a waste of energy. This effectively meant Christians should opt out of engagement with the state and not hold authorities to account. In effect, they abdicated their responsibility to be salt and light in society.

However, Augustine believed that the church could force people to behave virtuously. Given that the political rulers of his day were Christians, he reasoned that the church could apply coercion through the laws and discipline of the state. He therefore sanctioned the persecution of heretics by the state and supported extensive moral prescriptions within state law, with punishment for disobedience.

Both Augustine's and Constantine's (and Theodosius') models form the basis of two of the main views held by Christians today with regard to engaging with the state. The first, in the tradition of Constantine, is for the church to try and get as close to power as possible, to declare a Christian nation with an established church and for the church to use the state apparatus to achieve its own ends. The second, following Augustine, is for the church to concern itself with matters in the city of God, and only venture into the earthly city to protect it's own interests.

The Middle Ages: Islam, the Pope and Orthodoxy

Rise of Islam

At the start of the seventh century, according to Islamic history, Mohammed received revelations from Allah and in AD 622 he established the first Muslim community in Medina (Saudi Arabia). Within 100 years many other places – including Palestine, Egypt, Syria and Persia – were defeated by Arab armies and became Muslim states. The Arab conquerors did not separate state and religion so these new countries became Muslim, resulting in persecution of the church and non-Muslims. Churches in these countries collapsed under this persecution and the centre of gravity of the church moved north and west into Europe. Muslims were not only seen as a political threat; they also occupied the most sacred sites of Christian pilgrimage in Palestine. These, and other factors, led to the crusades, which were attempts to reclaim Christian lands and spread Christianity by the might of the sword.

Spread of Eastern Orthodoxy

The Roman Empire diminished in the east and this left a much smaller Greek-speaking Byzantine Empire. There were still links with the west, but Christianity was becoming more dependent on ritual, liturgy and icons than the intellectual or moral western Catholicism. This Byzantine Empire was the cultural centre of its day and by the end of the ninth century icons were accepted as central to eastern worship. Orthodoxy spread to Bulgaria, Serbia and Romania and by the end of the tenth century it took hold further east in Russia, where it was established as the state religion (which it remained until 1917). The Orthodox Church became established as the state religion and saw itself as the 'true church' in a similar way to Catholicism in the west. Under these Orthodox states, as in Western Europe, there was one established church and this ruled in tandem with the political powers, using state powers to spread adherence and obedience. Any dissention against the political authorities was therefore also dissention against the church authorities and was not tolerated. Freedom of conscience was severely restricted.

Power of the Pope, the crusades and the Inquisition

By the eleventh century, most of Western Europe was considered Christian and the church and state were seen to be the spiritual and temporal aspects of the same reality, a situation known as Christendom. The papacy increased its strength and decrees were established that the Pope could depose emperors, could be judged by no one and was inerrant. Effectively, the Pope was the highest authority and had power over the state apparatus and the church. He even had power to produce decrees with the same authority as Scripture. The church used its military might to expand, to insist on doctrinal purity and to strengthen its control over all aspects of people's lives.

The political and religious threat of Islam meant that armies from the west set out on the first crusade in 1095 to recapture lands, such as Syria and Palestine, from the Muslims and to expand the western Christian Empire further east. Successive and bloody crusades regained key states or holy sites but, just under 200 years later, by the end of the crusades, Arab armies again ruled the east. In 1453 Muslim Turks took possession of Constantinople, bringing to an end the Byzantine Empire. From there they pushed on into the Balkans where they left a legacy that is still very much a reality today, as seen in the Muslim versus Orthodox aspect of the Bosnian–Serbian conflict in the 1990s.

This period also signified the growth of the Inquisition in the Roman Catholic Church, which saw the state and church working together within their own jurisdictions to punish heretics, usually with death. The Inquisition spread as far as the new Spanish Empire of Latin America and Lima served as the centre of the Inquisition for many years from the sixteenth century. Questions of theology to explore new ways of the church engaging with society were strictly prohibited within these established churches. Unquestioning obedience was demanded. Injustice could not be challenged because the church and state would both have been implicated.

There was also a renewal of monasticism, partly responding to the degeneracy into which much monastic life had fallen, but also as a protest against the control of the state over the church. Most of the new orders thought the only way to influence society for the better was by forming alternative communities, which were based on how they thought life should be and were far away from the reach of official church power. Some monastic communities followed Augustine's views on the separation of church and state, although others lived in the community, teaching and becoming socially involved.

The Reformation

Martin Luther and reform

During the Renaissance in the fifteenth century, there was a rediscovery of ancient (particularly Greek) cultures, and a growing belief in the abilities of human beings to develop and progress. Science, art, writing and architecture made great advancements. Theology benefited from this and many, including Erasmus of Rotterdam (who is seen by many as the forerunner of the Reformation), wanted everyone to be able to read the Bible in their own language so that they could read the wisdom for themselves: 'the plough boy ought to be able to recite Scripture while ploughing, and the weaver to the hum of their shuttle'. He was seeking a radical rediscovery of faith, based on the example of the early church.

At the start of the sixteenth century, confidence in the western Catholic Church as an institution was at an all-time low, with moral and pastoral corruption, papal extravagance and increasing questioning of doctrine. It was into this context that Martin Luther stepped. He taught that salvation was based on grace alone and not by works, and challenged the sale of indulgences where people paid priests for a shortening of the punishments to be endured after death in purgatory. Luther's *95 Theses* (on indulgences), written in 1517, provoked widespread debate throughout Europe and eventually led to his excommunication in 1521. His initial intention had not been to call for a reformation. Rather, he wanted a debate. However, the seeds of religious and political dissent were sown. By the end of the seventeenth century, Protestantism had replaced Catholicism as the state religion in most northern European countries, but in many southern European countries reformers were persecuted (e.g. the Huguenots in France).

Calvin's *Institutes of Christian Religion* became the foundation for Reformation theology and for the majority of Protestant theology today. During the Reformation much theology changed but the model of church–state relations remained largely untouched with the church and state still effectively ruling together.

The Anabaptists

Starting in Switzerland and spreading to Germany, the Anabaptists represented the radical wing of the Reformation.

They believed that the state existed for non-Christians and that Christians were to have as little to do with it as possible. They rejected the use of force, refused to serve in the armed forces or in political office, and refused to obey the state where they thought it contradicted Scripture, particularly over adult baptism. In fact, the action of baptising adult believers broke the link between church and state that other parts of the Reformation had not managed or aimed to do. The Anabaptists were viciously persecuted by both Catholics and Protestants, although these groups were eventually accepted within Protestant European countries, as were Catholics.

The Puritans

There were other groups who thought that the reforms of the Reformation did not go far enough. They argued that the state had retained too much power over the church. Some went as far as to argue that belonging to the church was a matter of the voluntary decision of an individual and that no state had the right to force this decision on anyone. Being a Christian was a matter of individual conscience and not state policy. The Puritans who advocated this position were known as Congregationalists or Independents. Some of them also advocated adult baptism and became known as Baptists. Because of persecution many fled to Holland, which was more tolerant than England at the beginning of the seventeenth century.

These religious exiles formed the core group of the Pilgrim Fathers that sailed to North America in 1620. They were followed by wave after wave of persecuted Christians. Among them was Roger Williams who, having sailed to America in 1631 and failed to find religious toleration in Boston, eventually founded the state of Rhode Island. The Baptists were advocating religious toleration as early as

1611, but Rhode Island was the first state where it was practiced. Rhode Island's policy that religion is a matter of conscience and that it is wrong to coerce people to believe in a specific way was eventually applied to all ideas and became one of the fundamental characteristics of western democracy.

The radical Puritans developed a Christian view of the state and political involvement that was neither Constantinian nor Augustinian. They believed that being involved with the state – the language they used was being a 'magistrate' – was a valid and important Christian calling. They followed Calvin's teaching on this, but departed from Calvin in their insistence that the magistrate could not use his power to force anyone to be a Christian in a way prescribed by the state; laws intended to force people's consciences were considered unjust. The magistrate was responsible for instituting just laws and for the defence of the state. This view has strongly influenced much current evangelical thinking.

Revival and Social Reform

Wesley and Whitefield

The eighteenth century saw a Christian awakening in both the United Kingdom and North America. John Wesley and George Whitefield were the dominant figures in England. Whitefield also spent much of his time in North America, where Jonathan Edwards had pioneered the movement. Wesley's open-air sermons attracted mainly the lower and middle classes and he attracted persecution from both clergy and violent mobs. His approach challenged the Anglican Church because he encouraged both men and women 'lay preachers' and preached in other Anglican parishes without express permission. By encouraging the development of personal spirituality, Wesley was, in fact, encouraging a more independent church that was removed from the power of office and state.

Wesley was also intensely concerned for the poor. This led to his establishing a huge range of relief and development projects such as clothing banks, skills training and micro loans. Wesley also wrote a pamphlet on the iniquity of feeding good grain to horses, which had pushed up the price so that the poor were starving to death. This personal spirituality and distance from the established churches gave Christians more freedom to challenge the way things had always been done and meant they could get involved in society as smaller groups.

The fruits of the revival were many. There was renewed interest in missionary movements, as well as increased emphasis on religious education and discipleship. There was much greater social involvement, such as workshops for the unemployed, care for widows and orphans, and provision of food and clothing for the poor. However, perhaps the most significant move was not just to help those who society had forgotten, but in challenging the system itself. The grudging acceptance of the radical Puritan principle of toleration combined with the enthusiasm of the Methodist revival made it possible for Christians to engage with the state to produce a better society. There was a strong impetus for prison reform and Wesley's vehement opposition to slavery gave a crucial impetus to the campaign to abolish the practice.

The Abolition of Slavery

At the end of the eighteenth-century, Britain controlled more than half of the world's slave trade. The slave lobby was powerful and active, defending their right to engage in the slave trade, due to the substantial profits it made possible. The planters and merchants carried on a vigorous campaign of rallies, petitions, and parliamentary lobbying to keep the trade going. Propaganda was placed in libraries, reading rooms, and coffee houses. Frightening estimates of the costs of compensating the planters were suggested and the risk of French competition was raised. Abolition would not benefit the slaves, it was claimed, because the French would simply take over the trade.

But a campaign over many years managed to turn public opinion against 'that odious traffic in human flesh' and to abolish slavery. Much of the work in Britain was done by the Clapham Sect, a group of Christians with strong support for the missionary societies but with a collective loathing for the slave trade. William Wilberforce was their leader and parliamentary representative. They were called the abolitionists. They had a widespread campaign, involving people from many walks of life, with hundreds of people, high and low, participating. Some invested time and energy in meticulous research, such as Thomas Clarkson, who was once reported to have searched fifty-six slave ships at Bristol until he found a sailor who could give him the evidence he needed. Others wrote pamphlets, lobbied MPs, collected signatures on petitions, organised meetings, and provided financial resources. At the heart of the campaign were local support groups and thousands of ordinary people, channelling information and adding their names to the petitions.

The abolitionists had to show that the trade was costly to Britain in terms of seamen's lives lost, and that there were profitable alternatives in trade with Africa. They also had to show that to abolish slavery was not only just, but also safe and would not lead to chaos. They stood against the government promise of 'gradual extinction of slavery'. In fact, full mobilisation of public opinion only came when the objective was radicalised to call for total and immediate abolition. Britain abolished the slave trade in 1807 and Wilberforce argued in Parliament for the enforcement of the ban and a European agreement to prohibit the trade. Wilberforce's successor in the parliamentary leadership, T.F. Buxton, believing in the necessity of an economic as well as a legal solution, made some compromises like accepting that there would have to be compensation for slave owners.

Slavery was eventually abolished in the British Empire in 1834. These Acts of Parliament did not end the slave trade for good, but they significantly improved the lives of thousands of those who were freed from slavery. The abolitionists continued for many years after that to make sure the law was properly implemented and slavery was fully abolished.

Missionary movements

The nineteenth century was a period of rapid missionary expansion, in particular to Africa and Asia. In fact, the colony of freed slaves established in Sierra Leone formed the basis of missionary movement throughout much of West Africa, with most of the missionary work done by the former slaves. Initially, missionary activity was closely tied up with commerce. T.F. Buxton believed that a 'Christian culture' would provide an alternative to the slave trade. David Livingstone, the explorer and missionary, believed that trade, agricultural development and the gospel could counter the slave trade and provide an economic substitute.

Many different church denominations were involved in missionary activities and these groups have tended to bring their specific ways of doing things. When many African and Asian countries became colonies of European powers, the political and religious institutions were set up in a similar way to those of the colonisers, with an established church that effectively ruled with the government and was given a preferential position. Even now, many of the most powerful churches throughout Africa, the ones with a privileged position and most access to the government, are Anglican.

All denominations tended to 'export' their views of political involvement or the importance of working for justice, whether this was an explicit theology of cooperation or separation, or an implicit theology of non-involvement, because of the lack of engagement by the churches. This theology has formed the foundation for much of the political theology of churches, particularly in Africa and Asia. However, most of the interdenominational missionary societies founded since the second half of the nineteenth century brought with them a sharp division between the sacred and the secular. They believed that secular matters lay outside the concerns of religion, which meant Christian often lived in communities that had little contact with people outside.

No theology, however, tends to remain exactly as it has been exported to a new culture. Many churches throughout Africa, Latin America, Asia and Eastern Europe are developing social and political theologies more appropriate to their particular contexts. Western churches have also developed new approaches to political involvement.

The social gospel

This was a loosely organised movement in North America from roughly 1880 to the start of the Great Depression in 1929. It attempted to formulate a Christian response to the rapid social changes of the period. Its origins were based on a strong link in the American revival tradition between personal holiness and social reform; a new concern for scientific study of social problems after the Civil War and work in Britain attempting to develop a Christian response to the problems of industrial society. Walter Rauschenbusch was the most important exponent of the social gospel. In 1917 he wrote *A Theology for the Social Gospel*. Having been a Baptist minister in New York City for ten years, Rauschenbusch claimed that all theology must stem from the central idea of the kingdom of God, believing that when Jesus spoke about the kingdom this meant, not the community of the redeemed, but the transformation of society on earth. It meant social reform and political action.[5]

The social gospel movement was most closely associated with both the liberalism of the time and an optimism about how far society could be transformed. It was concerned to produce a theology that was rooted in experience and relevant to everyone, hence the emphasis on justice and societal transformation amidst the appalling conditions in some cities and factories. Many evangelicals rejected the movement because of its lack of emphasis on grace and views on how far society could be transformed, especially in the light of the social conditions and moral despair in Europe and America after World War I. At the same time, however, themes of social service associated with the social gospel were also prominent among evangelical bodies such as the Salvation Army.

Since the 1930s the social gospel has disappeared as a movement in its own right, but its influence remains, both in the more liberal, mainline denominations and in the renewed social concern displayed by evangelicals since the 1960s.

The Twentieth Century

Many books have been written on Christian social and political involvement in the twentieth century and there is so much that can be said about it, particularly its decline and reawakening.[6] However, we limit our considerations below to five key movements that have had significant impact on the churches.

Pentecostalism and the Charismatic Movement[7]

The charismatic movement places a personal experience of the Holy Spirit high among the marks of a Christian. The history of the movement can be traced back to early Methodism and John Wesley who emphasised the 'inner work of the spirit'. However, the emergence of Pentecostalism came at the end of the nineteenth century in the USA when there was increasing opposition to teaching about personal holiness in mainstream churches, increased interest in 'spiritual' gifts and belief in the need for baptism by the Holy Spirit. Healing has played a major part in Pentecostal teaching and ministry, with exorcism commonly practiced.

Since 1950 the Pentecostal/charismatic movement has become a fourth strand in Christianity besides Roman Catholicism, Orthodoxy and Protestantism. Its main influence has been in churches in African and Latin America. In many Latin American countries the Pentecostals are the largest non-Catholic group. In the early years, Pentecostalism drew its support mainly from poorer classes of society in the USA, reaching a similar section of the population that Methodism reached in the eighteenth century. Significantly, in 1950s they were one of the most interracial institutions in the USA.

In the west (and in Africa), Pentecostals/charismatics have tended to avoid social issues, preferring instead to focus on prayer and spiritual warfare as ways of tackling issues of suffering or injustice. In many parts of Africa the movement has also been closely associated with prosperity teaching. In Latin America, some groups have developed a deeper concern for social issues and are working with many poor communities in social development and in tackling some of the injustices seen around them. Charismatic teaching has now influenced all of the mainstream churches so there are charismatic Catholics and Protestants all over the world.

Martin Luther King Jr and the civil rights movement

Martin Luther King Jr led the civil rights movement in the USA from the mid-1950s until his death in 1968. He upheld the right to disobey unjust laws, but was convinced that non-violent resistance was the most potent weapon available to oppressed people. 'Driven by his faith he saw Christianity as a force that could transform not only the individual, but the whole of society … his unique combination of the message of Jesus (love your enemies) and the methods of Mahatma Gandhi (non-violence) gave both a philosophy and a strategy to the civil rights movement'.[8]

Non-violent resistance brought on a crisis and forced the community and those in power to face the issues it had hitherto failed to confront. King's message to his white opponents was, 'We shall match your capacity to inflict suffering with our capacity to endure suffering. We will meet your physical force with soul force. Do to us what you will, and we shall continue to love you.'[9]

Protests included sit-ins, marches and boycotts. In 1955 King was pastor of a Baptist Church in Montgomery, Alabama, when a black woman named Rosa Parks was arrested after refusing to give up her seat to a white passenger and move to the back of the bus. King joined others in leading a bus boycott aimed at ending segregation of the buses. To sustain the protest, the Montgomery Improvement Association was formed and it organised a fleet of 300 cars to get black people to and from work. The boycott was declared illegal and King, along with dozens of others, was arrested for leading it. However, on conviction, King writes:

I was proud of my crime. It was the crime of joining my people in a non-violent protest against injustice … it was above all the crime of seeking to convince my people that non-cooperation with evil is just as much a moral duty as is cooperation with good.[10]

By the end of 1956 segregation on the buses had stopped.

In 1960 King backed a sit-in by black college students protesting at segregation in the student canteen. In 1963 he joined other civil rights leaders in organising the 200,000-strong march on Washington to demand equal justice for all citizens under the law. This was the occasion when he delivered his famous 'I have a dream' speech. The Civil Rights Act of 1964 followed. This authorised the federal government to enforce desegregation in publicly owned facilities and outlawing discrimination in employment.

King was arrested countless times. He lived under the daily threat of assassination and received mounds of hate mail. However, he was convinced that what he was doing was right and just, and that he had to go through with it no matter what. He knew where he wanted society to go. His role was to lead when he was able to and bring others along as well. King's power of love and conviction overcame the power of hate; the force of numbers overcame the force of the police.

King and the civil rights movement forced American churches to wake up to the reality of injustice and poverty in their society. Many churches played a leading role in the struggle, while others remained silent, staying on the side of the oppressive system.

Liberation theology

Liberation theology 'was born when faith confronted the injustice done to the poor'.[11] It developed in Latin America in the late 1960s as a response to the poverty that is so prevalent in many societies there. It was born out of the reality of poverty and strongly articulates the fact that poverty is contrary to God's will and that the poor can have hope for both a better society now and a transformed society when Christ comes again. But this is only possible when 'we struggle alongside them [the poor] against the poverty that has been unjustly created and forced on them'.[12] Liberation theologians base much of their social analysis on Marxist thought. They trace poverty and oppression to the concentration of power and economic wealth in the hands of a few.

Liberation theology developed in the universities during the 1970s and it became a populist movement with the growth of the 'Base Ecclesial Communities'. These were small, grassroots, lay groups of the poor or ordinary people, who met to pray, conduct Bible studies and discuss their social and political obligations. According to one commentator, 'in liberation, the oppressed come together, come to understand their situation ... discover the causes of their oppression, organise themselves into movements and act in a co-ordinated fashion'.[13] This has many similarities with Christian development that empowers the poor to be agents of their own change and has a strong educational approach.

Initially, liberation theology developed as a reaction to the conservative Catholicism in Latin America, and was the interest of a minority. It then became more a part of mainstream Catholicism, although it seems to have been suppressed again under the current Pope John Paul II. This movement has helped to refocus the worldwide church on the importance of working with the poor, on trying to contextualise biblical theology to current situations and on seeing the wider social implications of liberation that Jesus came to bring. It has also helped the church to see the poor and oppressed as agents of their own social and political liberation, not just as passive recipients of help. In addition, it has helped to give birth to liberation theologies for other marginalised groups, such as women, black people and indigenous people. These liberation theologies challenge previous theories of dependency and enable these groups to look deeper at the causes of poverty and marginalisation in their societies, and develop possible solutions.

However, in its focus on changing society, some advocates of liberation theology underplay the importance of individual salvation and a personal relationship with God. They are in danger of providing a narrow view of sin that is purely structural and not personal and of idealising the poor and oppressed due to the situation they find themselves in. In reality, an understanding of sin that is both personal and social is essential to understanding the causes of poverty because an individual cannot exist apart from society, and society is made up of individuals in communities. Churches need to guard themselves against either a wholesale rejection or wholesale acceptance of liberation theology. However, some of the leading liberation theologians do accept the need for personal salvation. This should be welcomed.

Lausanne

In the 1960s and 1970s the debate about social action and evangelism was raging. There were various high-profile international conferences, but, according to René Padilla, 'the *Lausanne Congress* [in 1974] may be regarded as the most important world-wide evangelical gathering of the twentieth century'.[14] A statement of evangelical belief, the *Lausanne Covenant*, was produced:

[This] not only expressed penitence for the neglect of social action, but it also acknowledged that socio-political involvement was, together with evangelism, an essential part of Christian mission. In so doing it gave the deathblow to attempts to reduce mission to the multiplication of Christians and churches through evangelism.[15]

Part of paragraph 5 of the Covenant stated:

> Although reconciliation with man is not reconciliation with
> God, nor is social action evangelism, nor is political liberation
> salvation, nevertheless we affirm that evangelism and
> socio-political involvement are both part of our Christian
> duty. For both are expressions of our doctrines of God and
> man, our love for our neighbour and our obedience to Jesus
> Christ. The message of salvation implies a message of judge-
> ment on every form of alienation, oppression and discrimina-
> tion, and we should not be afraid to denounce evil and injustice
> wherever they exist. When people receive Christ they are born
> again into his kingdom and must seek not only to exhibit but
> also to spread its righteousness in the midst of an unrighteous
> world.[16]

Social involvement and evangelism were therefore seen as
integral parts of the mission of the church. Many churches
have embraced this understanding, although far too many
still see a conflict.

Shifting centre of gravity

One of the most significant changes at the start of the
twenty-first century is that the centre of gravity of Christianity has moved from the west to Africa, Latin America
and Asia. This is clearly the case numerically, and many
national and indigenous churches have contextualised the
gospel for their situations. The Lausanne Conference
started to bring much more theology from different parts of
the world to influence theology in the west and this brought
a greater emphasis on problems such as poverty and social
injustice. The dominant tide of liberation theology in Latin
America also caused western evangelicals to look more
closely at theology being developed around the world.

There is also an increasing awareness of the moral decline in many western societies, so Christians in developing countries are learning from past mistakes of the church and trying to ensure that the church avoids many of the mistakes in the west, such as being too close to political power or too focused on the middle classes and wealthy sections of society. These experiences can only help to enrich the global church as it seeks to be faithful to its mission and to be 'good news to the poor'.

Conclusion

There is a long history of socio-political involvement of the church and of individual Christians. In many circumstances Christians have led the way in social reform. In others they have, unfortunately, been on the side of the oppressors or simply silent in the face of injustice. These responses have usually been defined by particular political theologies and contexts. This again emphasises the importance of having a correct biblical understanding of the role of the church and of the state in bringing about God's kingdom. As both socio-political action and evangelism are increasingly accepted as integral parts of the same gospel, the challenge to each of us as Christians is to build on our rich heritage and become involved in the transformation of our societies. What could happen if you got involved?

Questions for Reflection

- What 'political' role do you think the church has in your country? Do you think the church should seek to be established or disestablished by the state?
- How is the political theology of your church influenced by church history?

- How has the church in your country engaged with politics in the past twenty years? Do you agree with this approach? What has been good and bad about this approach?
- What safeguards can the church put in place to stop it being compromised when becoming involved in political activity?

Further Reading

Augustine, *Political Writings*

Boff, Leonardo and Clodovis Boff, *Introducing Liberation Theology*

Carson, Clayborne (ed.), *The Autobiography of Martin Luther King Jr*

Chester, Tim (ed.), *Justice, Mercy and Humility: Integral Mission and the Poor*

Lion Handbook, *The History of Christianity*

Stott, John, *Making Christ Known: Historic Mission Documents from the Lausanne Movement, 1974–1989*

Stott, John, *New Issues Facing Christians Today*

Wallis, Jim, *The Soul of Politics: A Practical and Prophetic Vision for Change*

Section 2

Experiences from Around the World

Experiences from Around the World

7

Reconciliation and Healing: Rwanda[1]

Introduction

No one can fail to be horrified by the events of 1994 when, in 100 days, the Hutu militia, (the *interahamwe*), killed between 800,000 and one million Tutsis and moderate Hutus. This chapter does not try to give a detailed account of what happened or answer questions of why or how. It simply tells the stories of Christians who stood against the dominant tide of hatred and of organisations and individuals that are now working to bring reconciliation. It is clear that much still needs to be done in Rwanda and the genocide will affect generations to come. There are thousands who are still suffering deeply from the events, many who are unrepentant of their involvement and others who still harbour hatred and the desire for revenge. That being said, God is one who restores and reconciles. There are signs of hope in Rwanda.

Practical Reconciliation

Immediately after the genocide, the whole country faced the same problems. There was widespread poverty and a lack of food and safe water, land and homes were destroyed (particularly property belonging to the Tutsis), there were thousands of widows and orphans, and the infrastructure had ground to a halt. There were very few pastors or bishops to lead the churches. They had either been killed or gone into exile. There was deep suspicion among communities. Hutus feared revenge by Tutsis, and most Tutsis considered all Hutus guilty and thus hated them. At this time, the Hutu and Tutsi communities were physically quite separate because Tutsis were in towns where they could find accommodation and security close to the army.

It was into this situation that both the Rural Development Interdiocesan Service (RDIS) and Moucecore, two Christian organisations concerned with reconciliation and the reconstruction of Rwanda, started working. Michel Kayitaba, a man with a single-minded determination to bring reconciliation throughout the country, heads up Moucecore. He is a Tutsi and his entire extended family were killed during the genocide, leaving only him, his wife and children. He remained in Rwanda the entire time and was hidden by six different Hutu families, some of whom were willing to die for him rather than allow him to be killed. As a result, he says, 'I am grateful that I ended the war without hatred towards the Hutus.'

After the genocide, the first place Michel went to was his home town in Kigeme Diocese in the northwest, preaching a message of repentance and reconciliation to the predominantly Hutu population there. Referring to Philippians 3:13, 'forgetting what is behind and straining towards what is ahead', he encouraged people to look to the future in order to find life. Michel also spoke openly about the events between Tutsis and Hutus when few dared to speak publicly of what had happened. Returning from this first trip, Michel found that he had raised suspicions among Tutsi friends who accused him of betraying them by staying with a Hutu family. This was a characteristic response to many of those who had the courage to speak out soon after the genocide. Nevertheless, Michel stood firm in the certainty of his calling and vision: 'The *interahamwe* spread hatred and destruction. We want to reverse what they did and teach a positive message of reconciliation to spread across the whole country.'

From small beginnings, Moucecore now has a national influence. They train people at a national level who in turn train others to work with the local community. At a parish level, groups concentrate on an economic activity to cement their relationships and enable them to see the tangible benefits of reconciliation. This economic activity shows that people need each other and that reconciliation is more than just changing feelings towards others, but is living and working with them for mutual benefit. This work has enabled the local church to take its rightful place at the centre of reconciliation.

Brief history

There are three main ethnic groups in Rwanda: Hutus (85–90 per cent), Tutsis (10–15 per cent) and Twa (~1 per cent). As a Belgian colony, the Tutsis were given preferential treatment until 1959 when the Belgians started to favour the Hutus. In the years immediately following this, an estimated 250,000 Tutsis fled to Uganda and Burundi to escape persecution. In 1972 there was a Hutu uprising next door in Burundi and many Hutus fled to Rwanda. The resulting instability meant that Tutsis were again the target of state violence. Another 100,000 fled. Over the years tens of thousands of others fled in smaller groups. In 1990 there was an invasion from Uganda of the Tutsi-led RPF (Rwandan Patriotic Front), which was repelled. However, the government took it as a pretext to start killing Tutsis inside the country.

During 1991–94 there were various unsuccessful attempts at brokering a ceasefire and power-sharing agreement. These ended on 6 April 1994 when a plane was shot down. It was carrying the

Hutu President of Rwanda, Habyarimana, who was on the way back from trying to broker a peace agreement. Hutu militia accused Tutsis of being responsible. The massacres began within an hour of the plane crash.

In early July 1994 the RPF invaded the country from Uganda, and quickly formed the Government of National Unity. 750,000 Tutsis came back into the country over the following nine months. At the same time, up to two million Hutus, fearing repercussions, fled to Zaire, Tanzania and Burundi. Within the first year after the genocide, 500,000 returned from Zaire. In November 1996 a further 700,000 returned and one month later a further 500,000 returned from Tanzania.

RDIS, working in the southwest, held a series of workshops. Participants started by drawing a historical timeline of the main events since 1959 and, for each key event, they had to imagine themselves first as one group and then as the other. They had to answer various questions. For example, what did you suffer? What did you lose? What mistakes did you make? Through talking of loss and suffering they began to understand each other's point of view. They then had to explain why they had acted in the way they had. Inevitably, people spoke of mistrust, hatred, fear, desire for revenge and feeling mistreated.

Once people were aware of their role in the past, they were receptive to teaching on healing and reconciliation. First, people would repent before God for their role in the genocide, whether that involved hatred, standing by when injustices were happening, acts of revenge or looting, etc. They would then seek forgiveness and reconciliation with others present. Those who embraced this message then focused on what practical action was needed to rebuild the communities. These people formed associations of twenty to thirty people based around the church, who became like a reconciled community of people working together and supporting each other, e.g. in building houses, farming land, and developing industries.

Impacts

At the end of 1994, Moucecore came to Mwali, a village in the Gitarama province, which is in the centre of the country. Hutus were suffering repercussions for actions of the *génocidiares* (those who were responsible for genocide). The Tutsis had lost hope and mistrusted everyone. For safety they were living away from the community in the nearest town. Moucecore gathered together a group of Hutus at the church and, after analysing the problems they faced they started to plan how to practically rebuild their community. The first action was to try and reduce the anger of those who were suffering. Juvenal Mucyera, one of the community members who is now a trainer, explained, 'Talking was not enough but practical action was needed.' One of the first activities was for Hutus to return tiles, kitchen utensils and furniture to houses from which they had taken them. The church members started this but it soon spread to other community members. Next, the group started to rebuild homes that had been destroyed, starting with those that still had walls. They also planted crops in the fields for Tutsis who didn't have land or who hadn't been able to farm the land. According to Juvenal, 'When Tutsi survivors saw what had been done, it brought some hope to them and they understood that not all Hutus were killers.'

Consolate Uwera, a Tutsi who had suffered during the genocide, explained the difference it made to her:

All my houses were destroyed, everything was looted and they killed my family members. Fortunately, when genocide had started I had received Jesus Christ as my Saviour and felt the need to forgive. After the war we were in town but were told by the Hutus in the village that life is coming back to normal and the churches have reopened so we went back to the village. Later I gave testimony in church about how Hutu brothers had rebuilt my house and how I could forgive the killers. I went back to my house and invited all of the church members to celebrate and spoke publicly to forgive everyone who had wronged me.

It is clear that this reconciliation was only possible through God's grace. It is what Philip Yancey calls 'breaking the cycle of ungrace'.[2] Someone has to initiate the forgiveness and stop the ongoing hatred to make reconciliation possible. The person who does this may be ostracised, but it is part of the calling of Christians to be at the forefront of forgiveness and peacemaking.

Francoise Nyirankundwa, a Tutsi returnee from the Congo, explained the effects of a project that Moucecore had helped with in Ruhengeri in the north west:

When I arrived there I would not go out in the dark because I was convinced that all Hutus were killers. I welcomed the trainers from Moucecore, but still kept in mind that all Hutus were enemies. However, the trainers started talking about repentance and reconciliation. I saw that my mother-in-law was a beneficiary of a house built by a Hutu group. I also saw that group members helped an old Hutu woman to build her house and grow bananas, and that they were even taking food to the prisoners and sharing crops with the returnees who didn't have much land. Trust is coming back between the different ethnic groups as we are seeing God's work and understanding that we are all God's children.

Working in Prisons

Many people are kept in local prisons due to the overspill from national prisons. The association at Mwali frequently visits the prison and brings food to prisoners (who are dependent on food from family and friends as the prison doesn't provide any). At the start, many prisoners were still very angry, thinking that they had made a mistake not to kill all of the Tutsis. However, despite initial hostility, many began to become more receptive, and were challenged by the fact that Tutsis and Hutus were coming together to bring them food. They also heard testimonies of forgiveness from the group. The Hutu wives of prisoners also came, together with Tutsi women, as visible evidence that suspicion had been removed. The group were given permission to preach in two local prisons. Out of 1000 men, 100 have become Christians and there is an active church in both prisons. Some prisoners wrote letters to the community asking them to keep the unity and promising that when they are released they would come back and help maintain the unity that has been started. There is also wisdom in working in the prisons. As Juvenal explained, 'If we don't talk to prisoners, once released they will come and spoil what we have started.'

Re-establishing trust like this in communities has taken a long time and there is still a long way to go. What has been achieved so far was only possible when a community both faced up to its past and started taking responsibility for its future with practical steps towards reconciliation. This showed that community members needed each other.

Taking a Stand

Antoine Rutayisire is the head of African Evangelistic Enterprise (AEE) in Rwanda and talks about their work in stark terms:

If you decide to become involved in a ministry of reconciliation, death is one of the options. If you decide to be a reconciler, you decide to be unpopular. However, we are not working for popularity, but for the healing of a nation.

This has been a reality for AEE. In the months leading up to the genocide, Antoine was in a Bible study group with both Hutus and Tutsis, including the former head of AEE, Israel Havugimana. Israel was an outspoken critic of what was unfolding and, even when a petrol bomb was thrown into his house in February 1994 he said, 'If I disband the group because I am a Hutu and other group members are Tutsis then I cannot preach a gospel of reconciliation – I prefer to preach what I believe and to die for it.' He was killed a few months later.

Immediately after the genocide, Antoine started to preach on forgiveness but, again, encountered opposition. Politicians said that it wasn't the right time. Church leaders accused him of preaching a 'diluted gospel'. Forgiveness was an unpopular issue because people were filled with so much hatred. However, the government soon recognised that forgiveness was central for reconciliation, although the church was still reluctant to embrace it. According to Antoine, 'the result was that forgiveness left the church and went into the government'. He sees the church as having a central role in bringing reconciliation, but is frustrated by its lack of engagement at an institutional level:

The major problem of the church is silence – still. It has been afraid of controversy, of hostility and of taking a position. The church tried to be neutral, but neutrality is out of the question. You cannot be neutral when someone is dying. Rather than tackling anger, hatred and bitterness the church preached a neutral gospel of love of God or faith. This did not address the reality of the situation and created a large number of bystanders who allowed evil to be perpetrated. The church as an institution failed the country. It did not stand up for the weak. It simply stood with the powerful and that was a failure. This is not just the church in Rwanda, but globally. Now, if the country is going to be reconciled, Christians need to stand in the gap.

He compares the church to the twelve disciples when Jesus was arrested: one betrayed Jesus; nine ran away; one followed at a distance and denied that he knew Jesus. Only one stood at the foot of the cross.

Moucecore and AEE insist that people have to talk about the past and speak the truth otherwise they will just be storing up problems for later and there will be no forgiveness, repentance and reconciliation. The action of bringing things out into the open is essential to enable people to face up to what had happened and to their role in it, as opposed to burying it deep within them and still carrying around hatred, anger and the desire for revenge. Antoine says, 'sometimes people confuse peaceful co-existence with reconciliation. We may live peacefully together but hating each other. That is not reconciliation and will backfire in the future.' Violette Nyirarukundo, a trauma counsellor, told me that 'you have to let the hearts bleed so they can be healed. If you cover them up too quickly they will either turn bad or explode.'

AEE aims to spread this message of reconciliation as widely as possible, not just in the churches. Every Friday they transmit a radio programme on the national radio. Each week they make the programme topical (e.g. for the *Gacaca* courts [see below] they outlined the issues people would be facing and gave them a biblical perspective). Millions of people heard this radio broadcast and Antoine was asked to be on the National Commission for Unity and Reconciliation, where he is now vice chair and is heavily involved in the *Gacaca* system and in the release and re-education of prisoners. Due to the stand that he had taken previously and his tireless efforts at the local level, he has been able to influence policies at the national level that will affect the direction and type of justice throughout the whole country.

Gacaca Justice

The *Gacaca* are traditional community courts in which the whole community participates in bringing justice. When these courts were first set up in 2002, there were roughly 120,000 people still in prison, most awaiting trial (only about 2,500 had been tried) and most of whom had been there for six to eight years. The criminal justice system was unworkable due to the huge number of suspects, congestion in prisons, cost of feeding prisoners and the lack of an adequate number of prosecutors, judges and lawyers. The government claims that it would have taken over 200 years to try everyone.

To enable the *Gacaca* system to work, the government categorised prisoners so that all, apart from the worst offenders, could be tried in the community courts. Category 1 (a total of 2,133 people) includes the planners, organisers, instigators, supervisors and leaders of the genocide. They will still be tried in the conventional courts and, if found guilty, will receive sentences of between twenty-five years and life imprisonment, with the option of the death penalty. Categories 2 to 4, where involvement was less, will be tried in *Gacaca* courts. Category 2 includes those who were involved in killing, usually following orders from others or were under duress. Category 3 covers those who gave people up to be killed or who were involved in violence against others. Category 4 includes those who damaged property.[3]

The *Gacaca* process starts with the community collecting details of the population present in 1994, those who were killed, what was looted, what infrastructure was destroyed and who was involved. Suspects then stand trial by the community. The local judge places them in one of the four categories or declares them innocent (most of the suspects are taken from the prison to stand trial, although a few who are not in prison have also stood trial). Central to the trial is the opportunity for suspects to confess their crimes (they have to give full details), to repent and seek forgiveness from their victims, and for the community to forgive. This is vital for future reconciliation because those who have committed crimes need to be reintegrated into communities. They serve half of their sentence in jail and the rest back in the community.[4]

There are reduced sentences for those who have confessed their crimes before the trial and slightly less reduced sentences for those who confess during the trial itself. According to Antoine:

> The *Gacaca* is a godsend because at the centre of the process are the biblical principles of reconciliation. It allows the offender to meet the offended, express regret, and tell the truth. They are then entitled to legal forgiveness as well as personal forgiveness. It is a combination of punitive and restorative justice. It is needed to eradicate a culture of impunity, but people also need to be changed and reintegrated. People need to be shown that what they did was wrong, but given the opportunity to go back into community.

According to Africa Rights in Kigali:

> *Gacaca* allows for the input of all Rwandans who lived through the genocide. It offers a means by which they can collectively acknowledge and condemn the genocide. *Gacaca* ... opens a path towards atonement, through truth telling, for witnesses who were either unable or unwilling to try to prevent killings. For genocide perpetrators, too, there is the opportunity to

confess and ask forgiveness for their crimes. More than simply a legal instrument, *Gacaca* creates new possibilities for social interaction and engagement. It sets out to improve relations among the people of Rwanda, and between them and the state.[5]

The *Gacaca* is a bold experiment by the Government of Rwanda and there have been some teething problems. Although the church at a national level has yet to embrace the *Gacaca* process and mobilise its members to become involved, many churches at local level are key players. Those involved in local associations that Moucecore and RDIS have helped to establish are taking a lead in telling the truth and encouraging others to do so. One government minister said, 'If there is one thing we recognise the Christians are doing well, it is that those repenting and forgiving are those who have been touched by the gospel.'

Future Prospects

Compensation is also a thorny issue in Rwanda, and one that goes straight to the heart of the current reality of many people who are still suffering. Widows are still without shelter, orphans are still not going to school and many people are suffering deeply from losing their families and their livelihoods, and from witnessing such horrific events. Antoine claims that 'few survivors have been compensated yet, so they are the ones who lose out yet again. There will still be dissatisfaction after *Gacaca* if there is not adequate compensation.' According to Michel 'the government is poor so compensation will be low compared with what has been destroyed. However, other nations are expected to contribute. They are also responsible because they followed the events of the genocide without taking any action.'

However, most people are optimistic about the future of the country, and the fact it can get back on its feet. There is significant new building in Kigali – a sign of hope and a sign that people think there is a future worth investing in. There are also mixed weddings, something that would have been unthinkable in the years immediately after the genocide.

Antoine lays down the challenge to the church as an institution: 'If the country is going to be reconciled then Christians need to stand in the gap. Neutrality is out of the question.'

Questions for Reflection

- Is there anyone you know, who you can support, who is currently taking a stand against injustice?
- Where could the church speak out prophetically in your society, but is currently neutral?
- What ministry of reconciliation could you be involved in? What would this look like in practice?
- To what current events does the global church need to respond, either out of solidarity or to seek justice?
- Which one of the twelve disciples do you most closely associate yourself with, based on their actions when Jesus was arrested? What can you do to stand at the foot of the cross?

Further Reading

Gourevitch, Philip, *We Wish to Inform you that Tomorrow we will be Killed with our Families*

Kabango, John Wesley, 'Church-Based Rural Development: RDIS, Rwanda', in Chester, Tim (ed.), *Justice, Mission and Humility: Integral Mission and the Poor*

Prunier, Gerald, *The Rwandan Crisis: History of a Genocide*
< www.rwanda1.com/government/justice.htm >
Yancey, Philip, *What's so Amazing About Grace?*

8

Providing an Alternative to Prostitution: The Philippines[1]

Introduction

According to the latest estimates,[2] there are approximately 330,000 women and 70,000 children involved in prostitution in the Philippines. This prostitution happens in a variety of ways, including women working freelance on the streets or residing in brothels. In certain bars, women are designated as guest-relations officers, while in others they may work as dancers or waitresses. Massage parlours are often fronts for prostitution dens, and women and children are increasingly being offered in business or package tourism deals.

Women end up in prostitution for many different reasons, but most do so to try and escape poverty. Some are sold by their families (either in the Philippines or trafficked from overseas) and are kept virtually as prisoners in brothels; others have run away from home at a young age and found it was the only way to survive; while others have started out as a way to gain some extra money and found that it pays much better than any alternative jobs.

Whatever the reasons, these women find themselves among the most vulnerable sectors of the population. They are vulnerable to sexually transmitted diseases, including HIV/AIDS, primarily because they are unable to demand protection from their customers. They are open to physical, emotional and sexual abuse by customers, police and brothel owners. They are stigmatised by the media and by society in general, and often suffer from psychological distress. According to Samaritana, 'Although there is the perception that most women become accustomed to their work, in reality they must learn to cope using psychological distancing when with their customers, in order to survive the trauma.'[3] For those living on the streets or as single parents without family support, their children are also vulnerable to attack, abuse, poverty and illness, thus perpetuating the cycle of suffering.

Samaritana was set up in 1992 in Quezon City, Metro Manila, to work with women to give them the opportunity to leave prostitution, deal with trauma and be retrained so that they have viable economic alternatives. At the same time, the organisation is working with other groups to change laws that contribute to the abuses of women, and working with churches to help them to prevent prostitution in their locality.

Befriending Women

Those in the outreach team in Samaritana focus their energies on getting to know the freelance prostitutes working on the streets and those working as waitresses or guest-relations officers in the bars. They have greater access to them and can speak to them relatively freely. Jenny Galvez, Advocacy Co-ordinator, explained:

We simply offer friendship to the women at the start. We don't preach or offer them tracts, but let them know who we are.

After a while the women started asking for services so we sought a permit from the local authority and we now put up a desk every Saturday evening in the street.

This desk gives health advice and offers the women the chance to weigh themselves, take their blood pressure and seek advice on other issues such as pregnancy and sexually transmitted diseases. It also offers counselling for those who are being abused or battered.

After Samaritana staff had built up friendships with some of the women, they started to visit their homes and the women were often surprised that the staff were willing to visit and be associated with them. In fact, during some police raids, Samaritana staff were detained and accused of being prostitutes themselves.

Training and Education

Samaritana also aims to offer the women an alternative to prostitution through their skills training programme. This lasts for one or two years and the women are encouraged afterwards to go back to school, start a small business or get a job. This training is essential if the women are to have any hope of leaving prostitution. Those who have been in prostitution from a young age and were not able to finish their education have few employment alternatives open to them, so need new skills in order to make a fresh start. During the training, they are often tempted to go back to the streets because they initially earn much less on the training programme than they could earn in prostitution. However, even if they do go back, the women are likely to be more aware of the exploitative nature of prostitution and more aware of alternatives open to them, which is one step on the way to helping them to choose to leave for good.

Training is not residential, so it allows the women to live at home with their families and remain part of community life. The programme includes vocational skills, such as small-business management, health awareness, leadership development, and communication skills. Products that the women make such as cards, *batik* and foodstuffs are sold through Samaritana and churches they are in contact with. There is also the opportunity for counselling and the chance for the women to develop a stronger sense of self-worth by reflecting on who they are, understanding how God sees them and taking responsibility for decisions that affect their lives.

One woman, Donna, has been through the programme.

Donna is now twenty-five, the younger of two children. While she was growing up she lived with her unemployed parents in a poor-quality house in Manila. At thirteen she started missing school in order to wash clothes to supplement the family income and by fifteen she had stopped school altogether. Soon afterwards she went into prostitution, enabling her to earn much more money. At twenty-one, she came into contact with Samaritana and started the training course, but stopped soon after because she earned so little through the programme. A year later she returned, more determined that she wanted to leave her life on the streets. Donna finished the course and is now running her own business with the help of her family, earning enough for them all to live on. She is also helping with outreach to women who are still in prostitution. When talking of her hopes for the future she says, 'I want to expand my business and become an employer one day. I also want to continue my studies and go to a vocational school to study computers.' About herself she reflects, 'I have learned about the spiritual aspects of life and deepened my relationship with God. There is a big difference to how I see myself. I am a better person. Before when I faced trials I would give up, now I have learned to depend on God.'

Bringing Policy Change

'We realise that direct service is not enough,' says Jonathan Nambu, Samaritana's Director, 'we need to fight the system.' Samaritana has therefore joined with other groups as part of the Coalition Against Trafficking in Women (CATW) to bring about a change in the law to reduce the chances of women being abused or exploited.

Existing legislation is inconsistent and it discriminates against women. Prostitution is outlawed and women in prostitution are prosecuted. However, the law is unclear on the liability of customers and brothel owners. They are seldom prosecuted and usually get away completely free. In fact, sometimes TV cameras follow police raids of bars and the bar owners are not arrested and are permitted to cover their faces so the public cannot see them. In stark contrast, the prostitutes are arrested and anything they use to cover their faces is pulled away, so that they can be caught on camera and broadcast to the nation.

To change the legislation there are proposals for two new laws that deal with prostitution, an anti-trafficking bill and an anti-prostitution bill. The anti-trafficking bill will punish those who traffic women, men and children for sale into prostitution. The anti-prostitution bill will recognise prostitution as a human rights violation and will prosecute those who promote prostitution, including members of the police, government officials, customers, pimps and owners of establishments used for prostitution. It will also set up a national task force, consisting of government and non-government agencies, to fight against prostitution and to provide services for the victims. Samaritana has built up good relationships with a few key senators and has been in regular contact with them urging them to help pass the legislation. These laws have been waiting to be passed for six years but, at the time of writing, the anti-trafficking bill is just waiting for the President's signature. There is growing pressure for the anti-prostitution bill to follow quickly afterwards.

Samaritana has also produced a policy paper that is calling on the government to address some of the other underlying causes of prostitution, such as high levels of unemployment and poverty. If women do not have viable economic alternatives, there is a danger that prostitution will be driven further underground, which is why the government needs to have a twin-track approach of helping women to be freed from prostitution and providing alternative possibilities to earn a living. The policy paper also asks the government to undertake more outreach to existing prostitutes and to educate the public, the media and the authorities about the new laws that are coming in. It is no use having these new laws unless people are aware of them and they are enforced.

Building Alliances With Others

The CATW network consists of a diverse range of groups and Samaritana is one of only two Christian organisations involved. The majority of the groups are feminist groups and human rights groups, and they are focused almost exclusively on changing laws at the national level.

Samaritana does not have the time or the expertise to undertake this lobbying to bring about a change in the law, so they identified CATW as a good network from which they can draw expertise, but also contribute some of their own experiences. As Jonathan Nambu said:

Each member group has its own strengths and weaknesses. Some are good at research and others are good at legislative advocacy. What we bring to the table are stories and relationships with women in prostitution. The other organisations do not have the experiences we have.

As a network they needed to agree on the broad policies they would recommend to the government. One key decision was to agree that prostitution is not a viable form of labour. This issue split the feminist groups and consequently some were not able to be part of the coalition. The coalition has also needed to defend this position against attacks by some people in the media and has needed to explain that decriminalising the women involved in prostitution was not the same as legalising the trade itself. Working in this way with other groups has been a challenge. As Jenny explained:

> The feminist groups are cynical towards religious groups, thinking we are just condemning people as sinful. But after seeing what we do and understanding our approach, they accept us as an important member of the coalition. They have also been observing us and wonder how we manage to help women to make a decision to leave the street. Our Christian presence is now a testimony to these groups.

The staff have also learned a great deal through their involvement, and have undergone training on legal advocacy, in particular training on how to take down details of any abuses that they see or hear of.[4]

Working as part of a network has enabled more of the women who have left prostitution to participate in the campaign. These women joined with groups from CATW to march on 5 October 2002 to commemorate the first International Day of No Prostitution. They also joined together to march on the Senate on the International Day for The Elimination of Violence to urge legislators to pass the anti-trafficking bill as quickly as possible.

During this process, Samaritana prepared simple leaflets for women still in prostitution to help them understand the laws and the proposed changes and to help them understand the exploitative relationships they find themselves in. This has been part of a teaching programme on rights that the women have but, as their briefing paper states, 'Empowering women does not just end with them knowing their rights, but also teaching their responsibility to respect themselves and others and to make good choices in life.'

Mobilising Churches

According to Jonathan, 'Part of the challenge for society and the church is that prostitution is not accepted but it is tolerated. It is seen as part of the way life is.' Samaritana is therefore educating the churches about the issues in prostitution and helping the church to understand its role in the world.

There is an existing piece of city legislation that states that no entertainment and sex establishments can be within 500 metres of any school, hospital or church, so Samaritana plans to work with local churches to help them understand this legislation and to prevent bars and similar establishments from being built in their neighbourhood. If enough churches challenge the construction of bars this should prevent them being built elsewhere and should reduce the number of women who are working in them. Mobilising the churches has been a slow process and many are not yet prepared to do advocacy work. However, some are awakening to their responsibilities to the wider community and are becoming a positive force for good.

Future Prospects

Only if enough churches and local groups get involved in their local areas will there be any chance of reducing the prevalence of prostitution, of caring for the women who have been involved and of providing them with a practical alternative. There is an opportunity for the churches to help transform their local communities and to help transform individual people's lives. The policy change that Samaritana have helped achieve at the national level will go some way to achieving this, but policy change is only useful if it is implemented and for this, the role of the local church is vital.

Questions for Reflection

For your situation and the issues you are trying to address:

- Does society stigmatise a particular group? How can you work to overcome this?
- In what ways can you work with the local churches?
- What role is there for educating people on the existence of various laws and ensuring their effective implementation?
- What role does the local government have and how can you work with them?
- What are the strengths that you bring to a network? What weaknesses do you have that you will need other network members to support you in?

9

Freedom for Prisoners: Peru

Introduction

From 1980 to 1995 over 25,000 people in Peru died as victims of violence. Many were tortured, about 6,000 disappeared and over 600,000 were displaced. Thousands were detained by the government and over 18,000 people were unjustly thrown into prison, many of them Quechua-speaking land workers, living in the mountains near where the main terrorist groups (the *Sendero Luminoso* and the MRTA[1]) were operating. Many were imprisoned due to a combination of the uncorroborated evidence of one person and the presumed association with terrorists by living in the mountainous area that was their main base of operation.

The situation was made worse when President Alberto Fujimori, after coming to power in 1990, undertook a coup d'état in 1992 against Congress, overriding the constitution and imposing new laws on terrorism and treason. These laws introduced life imprisonment for those found guilty, faceless judges and restrictions for the defence. Under the 'repentance' law, if any terrorists surrendered and incriminated others they could invariably secure their own release. As a minority group, with little public representation or sympathy, evangelical Christians were often the innocent targets of these incriminations. Thousands ended up in prison. Many have been freed but many innocent people still remain inside.

Visiting Prisons

In 1985 two law students, Alfonso Wieland and José Regalado (both now work with Peace and Hope, the human rights organisation), went to visit those unjustly imprisoned.[2]

They met Pedro Quispe. He had been the lay pastor of a small church, 3,500 metres up in the Andes. His community had chosen him as one of their leaders, because he was honest, did not get drunk and was one of the few who could read. When the *Sendero Luminoso* arrived at his community he was singled out and forced to resign his community leadership under penalty of death. They commanded him and a few other leaders of the town to give them grain, dried meat and other food products.

A month later, an army patrol of about twenty government soldiers arrived. Someone had informed them that the *Sendero Luminoso* had been there and that the people had collaborated by giving them food. They had been told that the authorities of the town had decided to support the 'armed struggle'. The commander of the patrol ordered all the inhabitants to come out into the central plaza. He asked them to identify those who had supported the terrorists. No one did. Then he started to threaten them, firing bullets into the air. The children were crying and the women pleaded in Quechua for them not to be hurt. Finally, the commander asked the villagers to identify the authorities of the town that had resigned their posts. Pedro and a few others stepped out and tried to talk to him. The soldiers quickly surrounded them, beat them savagely and took them off to the barracks, where they were interrogated for over thirty days.

They were kept in dark cells and only occasionally fed, usually with rotten food. They were constantly asked for names of terrorists and their hiding places. They forced Pedro to sign a document stating that he was a political leader of the *Sendero* and that he had ambushed an army patrol, killing six soldiers. They took him from the barracks to the public prosecutor. Only then was he able to see his wife, Josefina. She was so desperate that she sold their family property to hire a lawyer who, in the end, did nothing to help. She sold her few remaining possessions and moved to Lima to be near the jail her husband was in. At the time of the visit he had been there over a year.

Through personal contacts with those who had suffered injustice and after hearing many similar stories that afternoon, Alfonso reflects:

> On the way to the bus stop, José and I were silent. The tears in our eyes gave testimony to the intense hours we had just gone through. That Sunday was a turning point for me. My life would never be the same, or my faith. My understanding of God had changed. I had been converted to his justice.

Freeing Prisoners

The initial approach of the church was support for the victims of violence with assistance to widows, orphans and those displaced from their land, as well as providing legal assistance. However, as is often the case, support soon grew to include speaking out against the anti-terrorist threats and publicly calling the subversive groups to end violence, i.e. tackling some of the deeper causes of injustice. Pastoral counselling was needed as hundreds of Christians were suffering daily in a context of violence and insecurity. Peace and Hope came into being to work through the judicial process to secure the release of those that had been imprisoned unjustly.

One of the most high-profile cases, and one that involved an international campaign, was that of Wullie Ruiz

Figueroa.[3] One night in February 1993 ten heavily armed police officers came to his house. They interrogated him and his wife for four hours and searched the house from top to bottom. They accused him of being a terrorist and of being involved in the killing of a shopkeeper. In Wullie's house they found a couple of envelopes belonging to a family friend that contained material considered subversive by the authorities. They took that as incriminating evidence.

That night he was taken away, interrogated for two weeks and put in prison. Later he was transferred to a maximum-security prison. During Wullie's trial the military judges, faceless behind their masks, took a mere fifteen minutes to make up their minds and handed out a sentence of twenty-years imprisonment for terrorism. This would have meant release in 2013. His was one of the cases taken up by Peace and Hope.

Making Global Links

For individual cases they were defending, Peace and Hope linked up with groups around the world. Alfonso writes:

> The participation of European organisations, such as Tearfund, Christian Solidarity and Open Doors, was of significant help in achieving success. We don't have an exact account of all the letters and petitions that reached the Peruvian authorities … but there were thousands.[4]

One of the lawyers reviewing Wullie's case said:

> The amount of letters, faxes and emails we have received in the last few weeks has been incredible … we have already filled several boxes and all of them will be considered in the petition for a pardon for Wullie Ruiz.[5]

Wullie also took great encouragement from the support he received from people around the world:

> Thousands of cards started to arrive from different countries: Holland, United States, France, Switzerland, England, Germany, etc and also South Africa, China and Singapore. All of these with a message for brothers in prison: 'God does not abandon his children. We are praying for you, your family and all those in prison. May God strengthen you and give you freedom.'[6]

The participation of Christian international organisations proved to be a learning experience for some churches in the northern hemisphere. According to Alfonso:

> I think that the process of educating towards justice begins with the particular, through real cases, and then extends to the general. In the end, injustice has real faces; victims who suffer in their own flesh the mistaken policies of authorities. And it is from these cases that we can teach the church about the importance of working for social justice.[7]

For many in the north, these cases were the first time they had been involved in social issues and, through understanding the wider issues of injustice, many are now active campaigners on other issues and for other people.

Wullie was released from prison on 29 June 1998 after serving five years of his twenty-year sentence. However, due to his criminal record, he found that it took months of bureaucratic wrangling to finally reach a point when he could continue his legal studies. Eventually, he managed to qualify as a lawyer and now works with Peace and Hope to defend others who are still wrongly imprisoned.

Wullie has helped to free twenty-one people from prison and during October 2002, four of the prisoners that he defended were granted a presidential pardon and released. The men and women had all been recommended for release as early as May 2002, but could not walk free because the President took five months to sign their pardons. Peace and Hope are trying to speed up the issuing of pardons and are also working with others to address the cases of an estimated 100 innocent people still behind bars.

As well as defending individual prisoners, Peace and Hope lobbied with other human rights groups for an independent commission to be set up to look at miscarriages of justice. An Ad-hoc Commission was established in 1996 and, if people were found by the commission to be wrongly imprisoned, the president could pardon them and they would be set free. However, the pardon was not automatic. Consequently, many people found innocent by the commission still remain in prison. Also, even when freed, prisoners still had a criminal record and found it difficult to find a job. Peace and Hope campaigned for automatic pardons once the commission found them innocent, and automatic annulment of their criminal records. They also focused on the long-term need for the whole society to seek pardon and for reparations for those who suffered. They are therefore seeking to change the laws so that pardon is automatic and criminal records are automatically removed, as well as to use the existing laws to gain freedom for those who are wrongly imprisoned.

Wider Policy Changes

Since their inception, Peace and Hope have managed to secure the release of 250 people wrongly imprisoned, using a team of five lawyers. Meanwhile, they have, along with many of those released, raised their voice to call for reparations for the time spent in prison, for loss of land, livelihood and for torture or death to family members.

By the end of 1999 the Ad-hoc Commission had reviewed 3,000 cases but estimated that there were 750 still worthy of investigation. However, progress was slowing down. In the first two years of the commission over 460 people were pardoned, but between December 1998 and July 2000 the President refused to sign any release documents for prisoners already found innocent by the Ad-hoc Commission. When the Commission's mandate expired in January 2000, hundreds of people were left stranded and abandoned in prison.

The commission was then transferred to the National Council for Human Rights, a branch of the Justice Ministry. Here it foundered, but when President Fujimori fled Peru in July 2000, the transitional government granted a further 200 pardons.

Seeking Compensation

The new President, Toledo, came to power in July 2001 and established a Truth and Reconciliation Commission. This commission, which is investigating twenty years of political violence, has a mandate to investigate reported acts of violence and to recommend reparation measures for victims, including compensation for loss of family members, loss of land, loss of education and livelihood due to displacement and miscarriages of justice. Part of its role is also to recommend any remaining cases that have not yet had time to go before the Ad-hoc Commission. At the time of writing, it is working on its final report.

Peace and Hope are helping with the investigations for the Truth Commission and will continue to defend innocent prisoners until they are all are freed. There is still much to be done and Peace and Hope will carry on tackling injustice and encouraging others to do the same. In the face of so much to be done, Alfonso's resolve is all the more certain:

> I think it is important to place the Christian struggle for justice within the perspective of the mission of the church. This is because I believe it is crucial to emphasise that the responsibility of doing justice is not only the task of one individual or specialised institution. It is the task of the body of Christ as a whole ... I am convinced that we, as Christians, have lost this essential aspect of mission. It is a pity to have given up, thinking that it is impossible to attain justice in today's world. You don't stop being a father, husband or wife simply because, according to statistics, the number of dysfunctional families increases every day. We don't stop evangelising despite the fact that the statistics show that only a small percentage of people are responding favourably to the message of the gospel. On the contrary, we work harder when conditions are more difficult. Complete justice is probably a utopian idea, but that doesn't mean we should stop fighting for it to become more of a reality. Our God has given us talents, gifts and abilities for our lives to reflect ALL his attributes, as we are made in his image and likeness. Let us be a reflection of his justice in our lives and communities.[8]

Questions for Reflection

- In the face of so much injustice, what encouragement can you take from the final quote by Alfonso Wieland?
- Do you know of any individual cases of injustice, either in your country or abroad? What could you do to get involved?
- In what ways could you practically help those around you who are suffering? How will you meet these people?

• What links may your church need to make with other organisations to be more effective?

Further Reading

Haugen, Gary A., *Good News About Injustice: A Witness of Courage in a Hurting World*

Ruiz, Wullie, 'Celdas que Alababan al Señor', in *Probados por Fuego: Testimonios de coraje y esperanza tras las rajas*

Wieland, Alfonso, *In Love With His Justice*

10

Christians and Political
Involvement: Kenya[1]

Introduction

In December 2002 Kenyans overwhelmingly voted for a
change of government. It heralded the end of the rule of the
KANU party, which had ruled Kenya for the forty years
since independence. There had been an unstoppable demand
for change and after the elections there was a mood of optimism. Christian groups throughout Kenya were involved
in different ways: encouraging people to participate in the
elections through voting, ensuring the elections were free
and fair, raising the level of debate and information about
candidates, and trying to reduce levels of electoral violence
that had so marred previous elections.

The churches in Kenya have become significant players
because a very significant proportion of the population
claims to belong to them. With this came great opportunity
and responsibility, but also many dangers.

Since independence Kenya has essentially operated as a
one-party state. This was made official in 1982 when the
constitution was amended. From then onwards the National
Council of Churches in Kenya (NCCK) has spoken out
about changes that are needed to the political system, like

the need for a multiparty system of democracy, and a review of the Kenya constitution.

During the 1988 elections, President Moi and his ruling KANU party abolished voting by secret ballot and introduced a system of queue voting (*Mlolongo*) where people had to line up behind their preferred candidate. In a country where electoral violence was common, bribery rife and a culture of impunity existed, these tactics simply served to intimidate voters to stay away or to vote for the government's preferred candidate. It provoked public outrage and the NCCK spoke out very strongly against it. In the 1992 general elections the secret ballot was reinstated and there were several parties contesting the elections.

As a result of the outspoken and consistent stance of NCCK some churches left, saying that it was too political. They formed their own organisation, the Evangelical Fellowship of Kenya (EFK). According to Rev Mutava Musyimi, the NCCK General Secretary for the past ten years, 'Many of the evangelicals had not sorted out their theology with regard to holistic involvement in society. Their gospel was focused on evangelism and pastoral care and some social involvement, but political involvement was seen as wrong.'

Election Monitoring and Civic Education

The elections in Kenya in 1992 and 1997 were accompanied by countless acts of violence and hundreds of deaths. NCCK and some Catholic groups monitored them, but had no power to act. However, in 2002 many more groups became involved to try and ensure free and fair elections. The results were significant. The 2002 elections passed with such low levels of violence compared with previous elections that even the most optimistic were surprised (although there was still some vote rigging, violence and displacement).

NCCK worked with a network of groups to monitor elections throughout the country. The church, with its reach at regional and local level, could use these links to help people register as voters and mobilise them to vote on the day of the elections. This helped to contribute to popular participation in elections and ensured that those who participated are more likely to hold their newly elected representatives to account in the future.

Perhaps the most significant impact was the monitoring of election violence. NCCK built alliances with other groups to cover the whole country, with each group focusing on their areas of expertise. For example, the Centre for Conflict Resolution focused on the Rift Valley where there had previously been ethnic clashes and displacement of voters; the League of Women Voters monitored women's candidates; and Tawasal Foundation (a Muslim group) monitored the predominantly Muslim areas of the northeastern coast. Virginia Maina, Advocacy Officer at NCCK, was involved:

> The programme was formed one year before the elections so we were able to raise issues of violence at an early stage. In each of the 220 constituencies there were three people employed from our coalition three months before the elections to start monitoring and reporting back. This was significant because most intimidation usually starts some weeks before the actual voting day. The presence of the monitors sent a message to candidates that every action would be watched and recorded and they would not be able to get away with it.

Another impact of previous election violence was the loss of income to the Kenyan economy. In 1997 millions of dollars was lost in tourism, with bed occupancy in Mombassa shrinking by 85 per cent in some hotels. Bribery and corruption also made it difficult for anyone to operate an honest and profitable business. Many business groups decided they had to act to protect their businesses from collapse or closure, so COPE (Coalition for Peaceful Elections) was born. Their main aims for the 2002 elections were to promote free and fair elections, to empower civil society, to hold election candidates accountable and to contribute to a culture of integrity, dialogue and consensus in national elections.

The first task was to make the Electoral Commission of Kenya (ECK) more effective. This body had been set up after the 1997 elections, but had been powerless to act. As Omweri Angima, COPE Programme Officer, explained, 'The Electoral Commission couldn't act against election intimidation because the state was responsible for the intimidation. It would simply have been closed down!'

COPE approached the ECK. Instead of criticising them for not doing what they should have been doing, they offered to work with them and help them do their job properly. There was no need to set up a separate body or seek a change in the law to make the existing organisations and laws function effectively. There was already an electoral code of conduct in existence. It had been launched in 1997, but was not being enforced. In theory, it gave the commission powers to stop candidates campaigning and prevent them from being featured in the press. It could also fine them for violent conduct and even bar them from participating in the elections.

However, this code of conduct was not available to the general public, and few people knew of the ECK. As a result, nobody brought forward cases of malpractice. COPE made 20,000 copies of a simplified version of the code and, with the commission's approval, issued them free to the public. This enabled the public to be informed about what should constitute free and fair elections, and understand what their rights were. It also demonstrated that the commission was serious about doing its job properly. It helped ordinary Kenyans to know that they had something by which they could hold politicians to account, which was their right under the law. With good media links, ECK also persuaded the press to cover the issues, highlight the code of conduct and bring the issues out into the open.

In the 2002 elections, the ECK fined the Minister for Home Affairs and various other high government officials for elections malpractice. This brought justice and showed that the commission really had teeth. It served as a warning to others who were thinking of employing tactics of intimidation or bribery.

Following the elections, COPE began working with the Kenya Private Sector Foundation to set up a justice fund. The aim is to offer support to those who have been subject to abuse of power by the authorities (e.g. awarding contracts based on nepotism, denied a fair hearing, illegal possession of land or any other form of injustice). The support will be available to help them litigate against the perpetrators of injustice.

Constitutional Review

Throughout the 1990s, the NCCK, along with other groups, clamoured for the government to undertake a review of the constitution. Just before the 1997 elections, the government passed a law that prepared the way for a multi-stakeholder review of the constitution to be undertaken by the 2002 elections. However, it soon became clear that the government was not going to fulfil its promise and was simply going to make the constitutional review a government-controlled process with a few handpicked 'representatives' from civil

society, but with no real representation of the citizens'
views. So, at the end of 1999, NCCK met with over fifty
other groups, including Christians, Muslims, trade unions,
women's groups, environmental groups and peace groups.
They decided to undertake their own review process and
write a new constitution 'for, with and by the people'.

Rev Mutava chaired the people-driven review process
that appointed twenty commissioners to gather people's
views and begin drafting the new constitution. The government broke up some of the meetings using tear gas and
violence, but the group persisted in their efforts, confident
that the government would not be able to stop the tide of
popular opinion. Eventually, the two initiatives were
merged in order not to cause chaos in the country.

Through this participation civil society groups in Kenya
had become much stronger, both individually and collec-
tively. They are now more aware of the role that they can
play and more determined to ensure that any government
runs the country for the benefit of the Kenyan people.

The draft constitution was published in September 2002.
It was at this time, according to many people, that the evangelical church woke up. In the initial constitution there had
been allowances for at least three *Kadhi* (Muslim) courts,
which could exist alongside normal Kenyan courts and
could deal with family matters such as marriage, divorce
and inheritance. In the new constitution Muslims had
suggested the institution of at least thirty *Kadhi* courts,
dealing with all matters of law, and also for the inclusion of
a Muslim Court of Appeal. Some of the Christians that had
not engaged before were shocked at what they saw was
preferential treatment for one religious group and decided it
was time to get involved. If they didn't become involved,
other groups would take the available political space and
push their own agenda. The main issue for them was that,
within a constitution that recognises that there is no state

religion and that all religions should be treated equally, one religion was being given preferential treatment.

Those who had been involved for a number of years viewed this quick re-engagement of evangelicals with mixed feelings. Some welcomed it; others felt they were becoming involved for the wrong reasons and would alienate themselves by becoming involved in the wrong way. However, Rev Mutava welcomed the re-engagement. Consequently, the NCCK started strengthening its relationship with the EFK.

The churches (including the Catholic Church) have now all joined together under a banner called the Kenya Church. They are undertaking a joint lobbying effort to influence the outcome of the constitution. The platform is much wider than the issue of Muslim courts. They are lobbying on good governance and accountability, the rule of law and poverty alleviation, as well as the equal treatment of all religions and issues of the sanctity of human life.

At the time of writing, the National Constitutional Conference was scheduled for 28 April 2003, when the draft document will be discussed with the delegates representing all the stakeholders in the country.

Evangelical Re-engagement

Even though much of the evangelical church had not engaged in politics, many evangelicals, either in the mainstream churches, or as separate groups, have taken their calling to change society seriously. One of these is Dennis Tongoi, the chair of Christians for a Just Society (CFJS). The mission of CFJS is 'to seek a just society that respects the rule of law, is governed by godly moral values, and practices principles of good governance'. It has a small secretariat. Its strengths are in building alliances with other groups and in mobilising its members to be active in which-ever sphere of life they can influence. James Mageria, a member of CFJS states:

> In our daily prayer we ask for God's kingdom to come on earth as it is in heaven. But if you want the kingdom of God to come to a place, you need to go to where people are and bring the kingdom there. If you don't go to parliament, it will be without the kingdom of God. And there is no vacuum. It's either God's kingdom or the kingdom of the world.

One of CFJS' first campaigns was to raise the issue of corruption in public life. On 1 June 1999 (*Madaraka* Day), to commemorate the day Kenya became self-governing, they issued pledge cards asking people to sign up to three simple pledges: 'I will not take a bribe; I will not give a bribe; I will expose bribery.' They distributed 10,000 of these cards to raise awareness of the issues and to encourage people to take a stand against corruption. They sent them to many Kenyans, including members of parliament, business people, churches and other groups, encouraging people to stick them on their walls and distribute these to their friends.

CFJS has also been involved in a campaign called BOMB (Bring Our Money Back). Launched in 2000, it aims to repatriate stolen public funds kept abroad. Following the elections of 2002, Kenya is faced with a difficult task, not only of stamping out corruption at a personal and institutional level, but of deciding how to tackle those who have robbed the Kenyan people of billions of dollars in the past. CFJS will be involved in helping think through the best way to tackle this issue and bring about justice.

In the run-up to the elections, CFJS held debates with three of the presidential candidates, including the two front-runners. They were the only group that managed to do so. Paul Wangai, a member of CFJS, explained:

We had good relationships with politicians from all parties, which had built up over a number of years. These relationships created an environment of trust so presidential candidates accepted the offer of holding a public forum of discussion with professionals drawn from the Christian community.

The debates aimed to help Christians assess candidates to see who was closest to their Christian values and who had a coherent vision for the country. Issues covered included health policy, the rule of law and the judicial system, management of public resources and land reform. To finish the evening, CFJS asked all candidates to make a commitment: if they won, CFJS could remind them of their electoral pledges after the election; if they lost, they could speak to CFJS individually.

Debates were broadcast live on radio, reported in the press and filmed for television. During the debates, all three candidates urged the public to take up their role in making the country a better place.

In terms of impact on the churches, Wangai was positive:

People could tell who was a credible leader up close. For example, in how they responded to issues of sanctity of human life such as abortion or judicial killing. They could see who was the best candidate and make an enlightened decision. Also, the Christian community recognised for the first time the powers it had and it encouraged many to vote.

In terms of how the government saw Christians: 'We were seen as a significant bloc, as professionals with integrity. CFJS was seen as a serious body at national level that the government can work with.'

Kenya has gone through particularly hard economic times in recent years. This is taking its toll on the church. Two churches in the capital lost money in property deals.

They served a bankruptcy order against the person who took the money and won the case, but the culprit bribed his way out of any punishment. Being on the receiving end of a corrupt legal system enabled the church to understand more of the reality of injustice that ordinary Kenyans experience. It encouraged the church to get involved. According to Kamotho Waiganjo, a CFJS board member:

> The church in Kenya is undergoing a transformation. It is coming to terms with its role in involvement in social justice. It has instinctively been involved in acts of mercy, but is suspicious of socio-political involvement. What made them change was a breakdown in social order that had a direct impact on the church, especially when land meant for churches was grabbed by others. Before the church was only involved in its own micro initiatives, but it now realises the challenge of social justice is so great that you cannot ignore it and that one cannot tackle it alone.

The Future

The constitutional process has brought the churches together and brought them together with other groups, including Muslims. James Mageria was positive: 'We now have better relationships so we can talk to each other about other issues that we all face, such as development or human rights abuses. Unless you talk to others you will remain suspicious of them.' CFJS also plans seminars between Christians and Muslims to 'encourage dialogue that will bring us to common ground', and especially to prevent any antagonism rising over some of the more controversial issues in the constitution.

Mageria is, however, cautious about the change in government that has been so readily welcomed by almost everyone in the country: 'We must be careful that we don't become emperor worshippers. We must maintain our convictions about what is right and wrong. The danger is that we will be conformed as opposed to be the ones who transform.'

Questions for Reflection

- Is the church engaged in politics at a national or local level in your country? If not, what can be done to encourage engagement?
- Has the church been involved in politics in the past in a damaging way (e.g. been too close to the government)? What can be done to learn from this?
- Which other churches, religious groups, etc, could you work with to bring about change? What are some of the challenges in doing this?
- What can the church do to encourage citizen participation in elections and the wider political process?
- What one issue could your local church lobby the local government on? How could you go about this?

11

Overcoming Disability: Cambodia[1]

Introduction

Whilst the media has focused on how a number of children in Cambodia have lost limbs due to landmines, about 2 per cent of children in Cambodia suffer from a wide range of other physical disabilities. These disabilities have causes ranging from lack of immunisations resulting in illnesses such as polio, accidents such as falling from a tree or a traffic accident to poor antenatal care, malnutrition and sexually transmitted diseases. Many of these cases of disability are avoidable and working to prevent them is vital. However, there is also the pressing concern of ensuring that those who already have disabilities have the best quality of life possible.

One of the main consequences for children with disabilities is that they suffer discrimination and are often excluded from mainstream society. Many are ostracised by their families, being seen as an economic burden or even as bad luck (based on the influence of Buddhist beliefs in society). They may be excluded from school for any number of reasons. For example, they might be unable to travel to school; their families may be too poor to pay for the books and stationery that their child will need; they might be unwelcome because some teachers are unwilling or unable to integrate disabled children into already large and under-resourced classes. The situation is accentuated in rural communities where poverty is more acute and schools further away (some children have to travel four or five kilometres to school). Other children may also exclude disabled children if they cannot join in all of the physical games. Adults may discriminate against children if they think they are unable to work in the fields or help out in the home in the same way as other children.

The Cambodian Association for the Development of Farmers and the Poor (CADFP) has been working in Chhuk district, Kampot Province, in the south of Cambodia to address these issues.

Addressing Basic Needs

CADFP are in contact with seventy-nine children throughout the district. Their first action when finding out about the existence of a child with a disability is to visit the child, get to know them and their families and find out their main needs. The very fact of visiting can be immensely encouraging because, due to lack of attendance at school and the large distances between houses, disabled children can often feel isolated. Parents are also encouraged by the fact that someone takes an interest in their child.

These children are given basic assistance by CADFP to enable them to go to school. This includes bicycles (most children with one weaker or even missing limb are still able to ride bikes), learning materials, such as schoolbooks and pens, and school fees if these are needed. In theory, schools are free, but often the teachers do not turn up for normal classes and charge for extra classes as a way of supplementing their very low salaries.

Simouy is a thirteen-year-old boy with malformed legs. CADFP has been working with him for two years. A neighbour said of his situation now:

It is so much better than before. If he wanted to go to school before he had to get on the shoulders of another boy. When there were floods he was put in a big pot and pushed to school. With a bike he can now manage by himself.

Children with disabilities often suffer from low self-esteem and many families think they are a drain on resources. This means many disabled children often do not look after themselves adequately or do not receive from others the care that they need. As a result, disabled children often wear shabby clothes and suffer from poor hygiene. To counter this situation, CADFP provides each child with a basic health pack, including soap and towel, clothes and scissors for cutting hair. This enables the children to keep themselves clean and increases their self-esteem. Consequently, they can be integrated into school life. They also have a reduced likelihood of further illnesses, which could probably not be treated because most families cannot afford to pay for the necessary treatments.

Children are a key economic asset and help supplement family income. Many children in the rural communities are therefore kept at home to work. These families would have reduced income and increased expenditure on school materials if the children went to school. Furthermore, due to the level of discrimination, it can be hard for those with disabilities to find jobs even if they are qualified, acting as a further disincentive to go to school. CADFP visits each family and encourages the children to attend school, explaining that this will make them more self-sufficient in the future. They also provide piglets to the families, as well as medicine for the piglets and training on how to rear them. The families need to pay back a proportion of the cost of the pig once it is reared and sold, but they can keep the rest, which will ease their economic situation and make it more feasible for the children to stay in school.

This financial support is vital for each family to help them overcome their poverty and make it economically viable for the children to attend school and finish their education. Even if the attitudes of the whole community changed towards those with disabilities, if the children do not gain an education, they will still be dependent on outside help in order to survive.

Educating the Local Community

One of the main roles of CADFP has been in education, to help the local community understand the situation of children with disabilities and to help them to integrate fully into community life. One of the challenges has been to overcome prejudices that people have against those with disabilities and perceptions that they are second-class citizens and are unable to do much.

Sam Ouern, Executive Director of CADFP, has a disability himself. When he first arrived in Kampot province he suffered discrimination and, despite his qualifications, found it hard to find work. After almost begging for a job, he eventually found one. A couple of years later he moved on and set up CADFP. Even this was hard work because community members viewed him with suspicion and did not want to work with him. However, after a number of years, Sam and the staff of seven people are working with many communities and are accepted and well received by them. Sam is a dynamic leader, who easily builds relationships and is a positive role model to the children, showing them that they need not let their disability prevent them from achieving what they want to do. His actions have also challenged many in the communities to think differently. One community member, living near Simouy's house, said of their work, 'Beforehand we thought that disabled people could do nothing so we saw no need for them to go to school. Now we understand their capacity so are thankful to agencies that have given them help and educated us.'

The children have also been included in many activities to recognise their talents. There was a Christmas show in 2002 and children with and without disabilities participated in a singing competition. Seven hundred people came from all around and, perhaps for the first time for many of them, the community saw children with disabilities at the centre of the proceedings as opposed to relegated to the sidelines. Two children with disabilities won the competition and will now be travelling to the capital to sing on national radio. According to Sam Ouern, the Christmas show demonstrated that 'children with disabilities could do many things in the same ways as other children, so their disabilities should not be an obstacle to studying or earning an income'.

CADFP has participated in various role-play activities with the children. The Child Welfare Group, a national network, has developed a poster showing positive and negative ways for adults to treat children. A member of this group came to Kampot and joined with CADFP to bring groups of children together to act out role-plays to understand what children thought about bullying and other types of abuse against children. CADFP ensured that children both with and without disabilities could participate, so that all children got to know each other as equals. Again, it also showed people that those with disabilities could participate on an equal footing.

Both of these activities were videoed and the recordings are being used as an education tool for other communities. This education work will now be much more effective because there are good examples of children with and without disabilities working together. There is also growing support from community members because they can see the effectiveness of the work and they have been included by CADFP in all the activities from the start.

Building Alliances to Influence Policies

As well as the work at local level in changing attitudes and in providing basic needs, CADFP has been active in influencing policies at the local and national levels. At a local level they have worked with teachers to persuade them to include children with disabilities in their extra classes at a reduced fee or no fee at all. They have also lobbied local commune leaders to ask them to work with teachers and village leaders to include all children in school and community activities.

Nationally, CADFP have been active members of the Disability Action Council (DAC). This is a council established by the government and is comprised of all organisations addressing disability. One of the current activities of this council is to lobby for the amendment of an existing law that states that those with disabilities cannot work as teachers or doctors. This law effectively legislates for discrimination and provides a major disincentive for children with disabilities to finish school. CADFP had for a long time been considering how to tackle this law, but did not have the resources or expertise to do so. They therefore used their involvement in DAC to persuade them to take up the case with the Department for Social Affairs, with whom they have strong links. CADFP was able to use their experience on the ground, and their networking at national level, to push for a change in the law that will have significant impact on the attitude towards disability and lives of those with disabilities in the villages.

This networking has brought other significant benefits. According to Sam:

DAC is the leading organisation to help us get to know others working in our field. These organisations bring good experience that we can use to improve our programmes. It also gives support in writing project proposals and reports, and helped us with our research.

DAC also has a wealth of technical expertise so donors will often approach them to find out information on organisations working with disability and to seek advice on whether to provide funding or not. CADFP therefore have no choice but to work with DAC, but how they do it is important. They could have been a passive network member but have instead made the most of the opportunities to persuade DAC to push for policy and law changes that CADFP have identified as necessary.

Undertaking Research

In 2002 CADFP undertook some research into the attitudes of people in the local community towards disability. They interviewed eight different groups, including children with and without disabilities, parents, schoolteachers, commune and police leaders, Buddhist monks and church leaders. They received advice from DAC on how to develop the questionnaire and how to schedule the research. DAC also helped to analyse the results and CADFP invited them to help present the research at the Social Cultural Research Congress in the University of Phnom Penh in November 2002. DAC has enabled CADFP to improve the quality of their research and to gain access to a wider audience. CADFP are now lobbying for DAC to pass on some of the key recommendations from their research to the government.

The research showed that despite the underlying fatalism most groups had a reasonably good understanding of the causes and effects of disability. It also showed that most people wanted those with disabilities to be included in normal activities, but that these children were still often excluded. CADFP therefore plan to share the results with each of the groups they interviewed and work with them to implement changes. For example, to encourage all schools to have a commitment to accept all children with disabilities, for religious services and festivals to encourage the participation of all children (including those with disabilities), and to work with commune leaders to find ways to help transport children to school.

Working with the commune leaders is an important step because they can pass on information from village to village. The commune leaders also give CADFP permission to work with the teachers and village leaders to implement changes in all communities. Including them in the research is vital because it means they can see themselves as part of the activities and in a position to bring about change, as opposed to being attacked as the cause of the problem. This is the same for the other groups involved.

The Future

In the future CADFP have plans to make posters and leaflets to publicise the main findings of the research and help communities to implement basic steps to integrate those with disabilities into everyday life. They are also thinking of producing a newsletter, written by the children with disabilities to inform others about their experiences and their hopes and dreams, so that the children can express their own views as opposed to having others speak for them.

Perhaps the most exciting plan is to put on a play, written and performed by the children who have disabilities. In May 2002 children from the local community performed a play to educate people about how HIV/AIDS is contracted and how to avoid it. Sam Ouern plans to do something similar to educate the community about disability, believing that 'if those with disabilities perform it will have even greater impact'. This again will show that children with disabilities have comparable talents to those without and need to be integrated into the community as equals.

Questions for Reflection

For your situation and the issues you are trying to address:

- What prejudices and discrimination do you need to overcome?
- What are the advantages and disadvantages or working in a network? What options are open to you?
- What are the advantages of educating and mobilising the community to address the problems? What are some of the obstacles you may face in doing this?
- What scope is there for a targeted piece of research?
- What role does local government have and how can you work with them?

12

Breaking the Chains of Debt:
Jubilee 2000

Introduction

Jubilee 2000 was a campaign to cancel the unpayable debts of the world's poorest countries as a meaningful way to celebrate the new millennium. It was inspired by the biblical principle of Jubilee in the Old Testament (Lev. 25:9–10) when every fifty years debts were to be cancelled, slaves freed, land returned to its original owners and justice declared for all.

The argument was simple: developing countries pay back significantly more in debt repayments than they receive in aid, an average of thirteen times more in the year 2000,[1] and this is morally indefensible. Many countries were paying a staggering 40 per cent of their national income on debt repayments, diverting money from essential services such as health and education. Debts needed to be cancelled. Corruption both in the financial institutions and in debtor and creditor countries also needed to be tackled.

Jubilee 2000 grew from an UK-based organisation with one member of staff and eighty contacts on its database to an international movement made up of sixty-nine national campaigns and a record-breaking twenty-four million signatures on its petition.² The drive for debt cancellation existed well before Jubilee 2000 officially formed as a coalition but the campaign popularised it to a level previously unseen. It has been a campaign unique in its size, reach and achievements.

However, the debt relief so far agreed will only provide an average 30 per cent of the desired reduction in repayments for the countries concerned and just over 10 per cent of this has been delivered at the time of writing.³ The battle is not over. Jubilee campaigners still want the full $300 billion cancelled that will enable indebted countries to get out of poverty. That is why campaigning, policy work and lobbying continues under the Jubilee Debt Coalition and will continue until debt relief is achieved that will enable poor countries to be masters of their own development.

The story of Jubilee 2000 is told elsewhere⁴ so this chapter focuses on a few individuals who became involved in this movement. It shows what difference it made to them and what difference they made to the lives of those who live under the crippling burden of debt.

Inspired Beginnings

Isabel Carter, co-founder of Jubilee 2000, was given a vision from God back in September 1994 when travelling across Africa from Uganda in the east to Nigeria in the west:

> We travelled from the green fertile land of Uganda, through Kenya and Tanzania, brown due to drought, over Rwanda, suffering the aftermath of genocide and finally on into West Africa where the tropical rain forest began. It was as if God was unfolding the huge variety and diversity of Africa and yet reminding me that every country was pulled down by the

impact of unpayable debt. The conviction came that the year 2000 should be a Year of Jubilee when these debts would be cancelled. The belief that this idea was from God is what motivated me to persuade others to come on board in the following months and gave encouragement during the early years before the coalition for Jubilee 2000 was formed.

On returning to the UK she met with others who had the same idea, some of whom had been developing it separately for some time. One of these was Martin Dent OBE, another co-founder of Jubilee 2000, who had been working as an academic and was involved in lobbying for increased aid:

> Whatever we did in the way of aid would be rendered relatively ineffective by the overwhelming mass of past unpayable debt owed by the poorer fifth of the human race to creditors in the richer fifth. I was faced with a contradiction that could only be resolved through a programme of Jubilee remission. We had to do this in a way that would create a new beginning and ensure that once lifted out of the well of unpayable debt, poorer countries would not fall into it again. It was clear to me that this can only be done through a jubilee process on the pattern of the biblical jubilee.[5]

This small group of people, convinced of the rightness of their cause, set out to bring as many others on board as possible.

Getting the Church Involved

This vision from God, the biblical foundation and the sense of a movement inspired by the Holy Spirit were the bedrock of the involvement of many Christians. According to Nick Buxton, Jubilee 2000 Communications Manager:

Churches were at the heart of the campaign and it was exciting to see them bring such energy. It felt like a spirit-filled movement cutting across language barriers and across the whole world. It focused on a moral objective, on a goal that was right and therefore the churches were willing to work with groups that were not traditional allies. The church sometimes thinks that by retreating behind closed doors it will stay pure and be more effective. However, Jubilee 2000 showed that by getting involved in issues of social injustice that profoundly affect people's lives, the church could show leadership and have a much greater impact.

For thousands of Christians it was the first time that they had heard a sermon preached on social justice. Many were awakened with a sense of moral outrage that people could suffer in order for their countries to achieve strict debt repayments, and they were driven with urgency to act. For others, the Old Testament came alive and more relevant than it had seemed before. Thousands jumped into action and became involved in a political activity for the first time in their lives.

Audrey Miller, campaigner and coalition organiser from Birmingham, speaks of her involvement as a spiritual experience. She had just reduced her working hours and felt guided by God to use her newly found free time and her energy and links to get involved:

It started very simply. I stood at the back of the church with the petition and tried to persuade people to sign up. In the early days there was a feeling that it was people's own fault if they were in debt. A lot of persuasion was needed to show members of the congregation that the poor countries had already paid back their debts due to enormous interest rates, and that creditors needed to take responsibility for bad lending decisions in the past. As people became more informed they were willing to sign. Others felt that this was Christianity in action and that they could support their brothers and sisters overseas. They saw links with the anti-apartheid and anti-slavery movements so could see their involvement in a historical context.

Ben Niblett, who was part of local Jubilee 2000 coalitions in Leicester and then in Leeds, recounts how he got involved:

> I heard about Jubilee 2000 in 1996 when I was in London and thought it was a brilliant idea. I was inspired by the biblical basis of the campaign. At the time I thought it was a long shot, but was still the most strategic place to work to tackle global poverty. Although we haven't achieved everything, through working together we have achieved so much more than I ever thought possible. There has been some debt cancellation that wouldn't have happened without the campaign. Some lives have been saved and some children are now going to school that would otherwise be denied an education.

Strength in Numbers

The aid agencies involved in Jubilee 2000 from the start were convinced that they needed to form a broad-based coalition at national and international level for the campaign to be successful. This same belief was held at local level and throughout the UK individuals and groups got together to form effective local groups to develop support and come up with creative actions. Nick Buxton tells of how the coalition formed in Manchester:

> Early in 1997 various different individuals from Manchester had independently got in touch with Jubilee 2000. We set up a meeting in Manchester, chaired by local MP, Paul Goggins,

and twelve people turned up. The talk focused on Manchester's role in the anti-slavery movement when thousands of people signed a petition. I suggested we needed an equivalent coalition now and that someone should volunteer to take it on. Ed Cox agreed to start the process and 3 months later at the launch of the coalition there were over 150 people present, with representatives from thirty organisations. One year after this forty coaches from Manchester came to Birmingham for the human chain. Manchester became one of the most dynamic coalitions with all local MPs supporting it and a strong committee steering it.

These coalitions gave inspiration and support to campaigners, from those who were completely new to campaigning to those who were experienced campaigners and encouraged that new people were joining in. This was recognised at the highest level, including by Gordon Brown, Chancellor of the Exchequer, speaking at the Jubilee 2000 final event in December 2000:

> Let me start by thanking this unique coalition for justice ... this coalition of which the history books when they are written will say achieved more standing together for the needs of the poor ... than all the isolated acts of individual governments could have achieved in a hundred years.[6]

Signing on the Line

Jubilee 2000 was a campaign that caught many people's imagination and tapped into their creativity. Chains became a theme, representing the chains of debt. Many actions were focused on collecting signatures for the petition. This had the ambitious aim of becoming the world's largest petition and, with over twenty-four million signatures, it is in the

Guinness Book of Records as the world's most international petition. The petition was an effective awareness-raising tool because the message of cancelling unpayable debts by the year 2000 was strong and easy to communicate. Within seconds people were keen to sign and wanted to know more and get involved themselves.

It produced creativity, such as vicars chaining themselves to railings for a day, pilgrimages around the country and people carrying enormous chains through city centres. It helped to take the message into the marketplace. One supporter in Mallaig, Scotland, managed to persuade all but three of the thousand-strong population of the town to sign! In Leeds campaigners formed a human chain around the town hall, blew the trumpet to announce the arrival of the Year of Jubilee and carried the petition in a rickshaw to hand it in at the town hall. According to Ben, who was part of this coalition:

> The petition was great because it was easy and anyone could do it. It was genuinely international and gave you the idea of being part of a global movement. It also helped us to get over a quite complex point in a way that people could understand – an achievement in itself!

On 10 June 1999 another record was broken. Tearfund initiated a Sign of Hope campaign, encouraging those who voted in the European elections in the UK to sign the petition as they left polling stations. The churches responded enthusiastically and a record 230,000 people signed the petition that day. Stephen Rand, Tearfund's Prayer and Campaigns Director and board member of Jubilee 2000, masterminded the campaign:

> It was fantastic to see so many church members active outside their church doors. One church wrote to me afterwards saying,

'It was the first time the church has been involved in petitioning the public. The team varied in age from twenty to ninety, most people being above fifty. The ninety–year-old and his wife (eighty-one and in a wheelchair) provided the most amazing double act in catching people leaving the polling station!'

Angela Ditchfield, a member of a the Christian Union at Cambridge University, helped to co-ordinate the People and Planet campaigning group there:

We printed hundreds of 'Tony Blair' masks to send to the Prime Minister and stood outside the end of term balls, parties and social events asking students to sign them and add a personal message. We also put together a huge paper chain and people stuck a letter on the back and a small coin, specifying that the money be used for debt relief. This was sent to the Treasury. It is illegal to throw any money away so we knew the civil servants would have to deal with each card individually. We knew it would make an impact!

The UK Government alone received over 9,000 letters, 300,000 postcards and 300,000 e-mails from UK supporters on debt in the year 2000. These petitions and letters had a significant impact. It has been calculated that for each petition signature over £4,000 of debt has been cancelled and for each £1 invested in the campaign £24,445 of debt has been cancelled.[7]

> **Debt relief has contributed towards specific improvements in indebted countries**
>
> * Social spending across all Highly Indebted Poor Countries is estimated to have risen by about 20 per cent.
> * Mozambique has introduced a free immunisation programme for children.

- School fees for primary education have been abolished in Uganda, Malawi, Zambia and Tanzania, as have fees in rural areas of Benin.
- Mali, Mozambique and Senegal are due to increase spending on HIV/AIDS prevention.
- Uganda and Mozambique, among the early beneficiaries of debt cancellation and increased aid flows, have consistently sustained annual GDP growth rates over 5 per cent and, in some periods, up to the 7 per cent growth reckoned by the UN's Economic Commission for Africa as necessary to reduce by half the number of people living in absolute poverty[8].

Breaking the Chains of Debt

The group of eight most powerful world leaders (G8) meet each year to discuss issues of global significance. In 1998 they were due to go to Birmingham and a small group of local activists got together to discuss how they could make their voices heard. This was when the idea of a human chain around the leaders was first mooted. It fitted in well with other events that were planned so the organisers started working with Jubilee 2000 to publicise the event. In the run-up the Jubilee 2000 head office tried to organise a meeting with the Prime Minister, Tony Blair, but were repeatedly turned down. However, when politicians realised the strength of feeling, the situation soon changed.

Nick Buxton said:

> We knew something big was happening. A few extra people were going to meetings here and there, coaches were being booked and we knew people's strength of feeling about the issue. However, this hadn't got through to the media or politicians. Birmingham was really when the movement went public. seventy thousand people forming a chain over ten kilometres long could not be ignored.

Once Tony Blair realised how many people were there, he phoned the organisers and asked for a meeting. Afterwards, Clare Short, Secretary of State for International Development, spoke out:

> The campaign to cancel the great debt of the poorest nations that prevents them spending on health and education and basic decency for their people is a wonderful campaign, and I was in Birmingham when people came from all over the country to say to the G8, the leaders of the richest countries, don't forget the poor of the world ... That demonstration did have an effect ... I want the people who came to Birmingham to know that they did make a difference.[9]

Audrey Miller believes that the chain at Birmingham was a defining moment for many people:

> They talk about the day with such affection. They remember how peaceful and celebratory it was and the depth of feeling held by all. They also gained strength from the belief that their voices would be heard. People don't remember what the leaders at the meeting agreed, but they remember the chain. The people had more impact than the leaders.

International Links

International solidarity was a strong part of the campaign and churches were able to hear first-hand stories from their partner churches overseas, to organise exchanges and to undertake joint actions. Campaigners were also quick to respond to situations of immediate need of fellow campaigners in the south. When fifty-eight people from Jubilee 2000 Kenya were arrested during a demonstration in Nairobi in March 2000, Jubilee 2000 campaigners from around the world sent letters and faxes of protest leading to the dismissal of charges. Brother Andre Hotchkiss, one of those arrested said, 'Without the avalanche of e-mail, fax, and letters that poured into Kenya, this thing may have pushed on for a longer time.'[10]

The Leeds coalition made links with people in indebted countries. In the coalition there was a Zambian theological student, a Zimbabwean nurse and a Ugandan priest, who could all speak from their personal experience. They met with people from Nicaragua and Uganda who came over to speak at public meetings on fair trade and other issues. Some students from the university went to Zimbabwe as part of an exchange programme and were able to feed back information about the situation on the ground. According to Ben Niblett:

> It kept us focused on the real lives of people in countries where we were campaigning for debt relief. People in these countries were also encouraged that those in the west cared enough to act and urged us to keep going.

Ongoing Involvement

At a meeting in one of the main Birmingham churches on the day of the first human chain around the G8 leaders, one speaker asked the hundreds gathered inside to raise their hands if they had never campaigned before. Over half of those present responded. It was their first event. These people are the new campaigners and most have continued to campaign since then. They have continued to push for debt relief and have also got involved in other issues, such as changing global trade rules and calling for a code of conduct for multinational corporations.

Jubilee 2000 Leeds has a core of people who are firmly committed to campaigning on debt until the issue is resolved. They also decided to work on justice in international trade, and have formed a debt and trade coalition. All the same groups are involved and they have managed to maintain the links with people overseas and with local media and decision makers.

The Jubilee Debt Coalition took over the mantle from Jubilee 2000 and is still campaigning for debt relief. Jubilee groups have been established in many countries throughout the world and are still lobbying and holding their own governments to account. Debt is now included as a topic in most international meetings. Governments and the international financial institutions know that they still need to offer more debt relief to more countries in a shorter timescale and that there is an army of people ready to hold them to account for this.

As one campaigner for the Mothers' Union reflected:

> I now know that I, and thousands of other individuals, have made a difference to the world through our involvement. I can now trust that individuals and their faith and actions count. That's a great encouragement to getting stuck into justice issues.

Thousands of individuals around the world joined together and made a significant impact. What had seemed like an impenetrable world of international finance was opened up to ordinary campaigners, who managed, by sheer determination and strength in numbers, to bring change to the most powerful global institutions. In the 1980s many people would have seen this change as impossible. In the twenty-first century, campaigners know that they have the power to bring about this change and will keep up the pressure because change is not happening quickly enough.

Questions for Reflection

- What local groups exist in your area that you could get involved in?
- Which issues do you care passionately about? Are other individuals or organisations doing something about these issues and how can you work with them?
- What can you do to raise issues of justice in your church?
- What local contacts do you have with the media or decision makers and how can you use them to bring about change?
- Is there one local issue that you could become involved in?

Further Reading

Barrett, Marlene (ed.), *The World Will Never be the Same Again*

Greenhill, R., A. Pettifor, H. Northover and A. Sinha, *Did the G8 Drop the Debt? 5 Years after the Birmingham Human Chain, what has been achieved, and what more needs to be done?*

< www.jubileedebtcampaign.org.uk/ >

Section 3

Practical Ways to Get Involved

13

Getting Involved:
Campaigning on International Issues

Introduction

This chapter is aimed at those individuals and local groups who want to get involved in campaigning on issues of social justice, but are not sure where to start. Campaigning involves members of the public taking actions, such as writing letters, joining in marches or signing a petition. This role of campaigner is essential to back up much of the research and policy work that existing organisations and networks are undertaking, to show decision makers that the public cares and to hold representatives of government, businesses and international organisations to account. Without this public pressure, demands can often be ignored. With hundreds of people all campaigning for the same thing, they have to be taken seriously. (Chapter 14 then focuses on how to get involved in local issues when you join with others and target local or national decision makers to solve a local problem.)

There is no blueprint to becoming a campaigner. Each situation will be different. However, below are a few pointers that have helped others to become effective campaigners.

Prayer and Bible Study

The first place to start is always with prayer and Bible study. Through this we can seek God's perspective on issues of injustice and his compassion for those who are suffering oppression or the effects of injustice. We can ask for his wisdom and guidance for the best way for each of us to become involved. Bible study will ensure that our actions are earthed in an understanding of how God sees the world and the role he wants the church to play. The first five chapters of this book outline these issues in some detail. Some key Bible passages on justice for study could include: Leviticus 25:1–55 (Jubilee justice), Deuteronomy 15:1–18 (the poor in the land), Psalm 72:1–4 (the justice of the King), Isaiah 1:10–17; Amos 5:21–24 (the prophet's cry), Luke 4:18–19 (the ministry of Jesus) and James 5:1–5 (warning to the rich). Others are given in the index.

Joining with Others

Being a lone voice in the wilderness is difficult even for the most confident people. When dealing with injustice, issues such as international debt or unfair trade rules can at times seem far too big. That is why joining with others is not only essential for drawing on each other's experience and information, it is also an important survival strategy! As one campaigner for debt relief said:

> I now know that I, and thousands of other individuals, have made a difference to the world through our involvement. I can now trust that individuals and their faith and actions count. That's a great encouragement to getting stuck into justice issues.[1]

The first action to take is to get together with like-minded people. This may begin with just two people, but even then you can encourage each other and develop ideas about how to get others involved, such as offering to take part of a church service to look at what the Bible says on justice, writing something in the local paper or calling a meeting to gather interested people together.

Local church

For Christians, the obvious place to start looking for like-minded people is in your local church. One option is to encourage your existing home group to spend more time studying what the Bible says about justice, becoming informed about the current issues and thinking about how to get involved.

Home groups can pass on the materials they have to others in the church so that everyone gets a chance to become more informed. Encourage your church leader to study the issues and to preach on them. This helps to avoid the tendency in some churches to relegate the issues of injustice to a small group of people who are 'dealing with that issue' with the implications that others, therefore, do not need to bother.

Local events

Another way to get people involved is to bring a few people from church to a local event organised by another group. You can meet together afterwards to discuss what you heard and to plan possible actions for your church. This can help church members to engage with the issues first, considering the logistics once they are convinced that they need to act. Sarah Garden, campaigns officer at the Fairtrade Foundation, is involved in facilitating events:

> We have just completed a tour around the UK for Fairtrade Fortnight. Four producers came over from Nicaragua, Ghana and the Windward Islands and they spoke at various events

about the injustice they face on the International Commodity Market and how it affects their lives. They also gave ideas about how consumers can get involved by buying Fairtrade goods such as tea, coffee, chocolate and fresh fruit; and by campaigning for fair global trade rules. It is inspiring when you hear firsthand about the difference your actions can make to the lives of real people.

Local group

Many organisations have local groups that people can join. These include specific campaigning organisations such as the World Development Movement (WDM); human rights organisations such as Amnesty International; relief and development organisations (that are also involved in campaigning), such as Tearfund, Christian Aid and CAFOD; and environmental organisations, such as Friends of the Earth. These groups may meet every month or two and will be involved in activities such as writing letters, sending postcards, manning stalls, asking people to sign petitions and being part of media stunts. The organisations involved will supply regular updates on their latest campaigns, including resources and ideas for action. Different members will be able to develop their skills over time, such as liaising with the media, organising events, giving talks, organising letter writing or petition signing. Details of how to contact these organisations are included at the end of the chapter.

Student network

Many people gain their passion for justice at university. Students tend to have more free time than most – time to become informed, to pray and to take action. It is also a time when people form many of their core beliefs and values that will influence their behaviour for the rest of their lives. People and Planet is a campaigning group that has mobilised students for years on issues such as international debt, unfair trade rules, and persuading companies to pull out of Burma (where the democratically elected government was denied power by a military dictatorship. People and Planet asked companies to boycott the country until democracy was restored.)

SPEAK is a network working with students and young adults who want to put their faith into action in areas of social justice. They have helped to form groups in many universities and to inspire thousands of students to to take action, develop radical lifestyles, share their faith and become catalysts for change. Angela Ditchfield was part of a SPEAK group at university, and is still involved:

> It has been great to be part of a close group of people to keep me motivated and ensure that I take action. The SPEAK group has helped us all to ensure that the focus is on Jesus at the centre of everything to do with campaigning and that our actions are motivated by biblical principles. It has also meant that we are able to remind each other to continue praying for God to intervene and bring about change.

Tearfund has created *student net* and works in partnership with SPEAK throughout the whole network of students and young adults. *Student net* brings students together, and motivates and equips them for action through prayer campaigning and ethical lifestyle choices. A magazine is published each term. There are also monthly action updates with prayer and campaign ideas and weekly e-cards.

Before setting up a group, it is a good idea to check whether other students on campus with an interest in these issues already meet together. You may be able to join with them.

Becoming Informed

Finding out about injustice in the world is easier than ever! Information is available on the Internet, in newspapers, magazines and books, through campaign mailings from organisations and from personal contacts. The challenge now is to know which issues to choose and not to become swamped with information overload. It is best to start with just one issue and to become expert on it.

Read the newspaper regularly so that you are informed of general events in the world. It may be that you start to keep track of events going on in a particular country, such as Angola or Afghanistan, or of a particular issue such as access to affordable drugs for AIDS treatment or the sale of military equipment to regimes that are oppressing their own people.

Join an organisation that you know campaigns on the issues that are of concern to you and campaigns in a way that suits you. Look on their website or get hold of a back copy of their publications so that you can be sure their information is accurate and presented in a balanced way, and that you agree with their overall ethos and approach to issues of injustice. Once you are a member, make sure you receive the campaigning mailings (some organisations also have special group mailings), and any other background materials they have such as books, videos or reports.

Look on the Internet to find additional material and the most up-to-date information. This will ensure your campaign letters or actions are relevant and topical and that they will attract people's attention. If you don't have access at work or at home, most libraries provide this service.

Use personal contacts that you might have overseas, or join with communities from other countries who have settled in the UK. If your church is linked with a church in Africa, Latin America or Asia, ask them to tell you how unpayable debt (or whatever issue you choose) affects their daily lives. Inform your contacts about what you are doing and try and co-ordinate some actions. Craig Smallbone, WDM campaigner, made contacts in the east end of London:

> WDM East London and Jubilee 2000 linked up with the large Bangladeshi community in east London to work with the campaign in Bangladesh. Together we launched the Bangladesh debt network '*dam te mukhti*' and spent a busy summer holding stalls at community events and festivals, a public meeting, a club night with Asian acts, a meeting with local MP Oona King and a meeting at the Japanese embassy.

Taking Action

It is best to start small and manageable and to build up into more ambitious actions once you have more confidence and know there is sufficient support.

Campaigns meeting

An obvious starting point is a meeting with interested people where you can discuss the issues and take any simple actions that have been suggested by the organisations. These actions may involve writing letters to demand that political prisoners be given a fair trial or are freed; signing a petition and committing to get signatures of twenty-five friends; or sending a postcard to a specific company saying that you have stopped buying their products because they are exploiting their labour force. These are often activities that can be done in one evening and people can leave knowing that they have done something that they hope will make a difference.

Someone at the meeting will need to inform people of the issues. It may be that group members alternate in reading up on an issue and giving a ten-minute overview. It may also be that you contact one of the organisations from which you have received information, in order to ask for a speaker. Most organisations will have a network of experienced people who are willing to speak on a variety of topics.

Amnesty International Letter Writing[2]

On 5 February 2001 Golden Misabiko, a leading human rights defender in the Democratic Republic of Congo (DRC) was arrested and held without change at an unofficial detention centre notorious for torture. Reports suggested that he was repeatedly beaten with sticks and that despite passing blood for two weeks he was denied access to either a doctor or a lawyer. Upon hearing about the situation, Amnesty International immediately issued an Urgent Action campaigns appeal to over 1000 people to write to selected ministers within the DRC government. The letters, faxes and e-mails started flooding into the DRC.

The first improvement was that Golden was transferred to a different detention centre where, it is believed, his torture and ill treatment finally stopped. However, he was still in prison without charge. He was still a prisoner of conscience. The letters kept flooding in and in late August the DRC Minister of State announced that all prisoners of conscience would be released. However, four days later still nothing had happened. Amnesty issued a new appeal and letters of protest were again targeted at DRC ministers. This time the final breakthrough came. On 13 September, Golden Misabiko was finally released without charge. He had been a prisoner of conscience for seven months. One of the first things he did was to send his thanks to all of those who sent appeals on his behalf.

Educating others

In order to increase the impact, it is a good idea to spread the campaign and get as many people involved as possible.

You may ask for a slot in the Sunday service (or even a whole service), or visit home groups and explain the campaign and how people can get involved. For churches, it is usually better to use existing meetings to do this, as opposed to adding another meeting that people may be reluctant to attend. Eye-catching posters or simple sketches or visual aids (e.g. drinking a glass of water with brown-coloured dye to highlight the fact that over one billion people lack access to safe drinking water) can help lodge the issue in people's minds. The education should enable people to understand the injustice you are concerned about and be able to do something about it. Leah Robson is involved in a home group in her church:

> Two years ago we decided as a home group to spend more time considering our response to the injustice we saw in the world. We regularly receive and study materials from Tearfund and have hosted fair-trade stalls as well as putting on a harvest supper where we heard a talk on international trade and world hunger.

One of the big challenges of campaigning is getting the message to the public at large. Simple actions, such as signing a petition or sending a postcard can draw people in and give them the opportunity to find out more. The Jubilee 2000 petition, which ended up being signed by a record 24.1 million people, did just this. It provided both a simple action to take and also the opportunity to explain the issues in more detail so that people could take further action such as writing to the financial institutions or the Chancellor of the Exchequer, or participating in one of the many stunts when people chained themselves together to signify the 'chains of debt' by which poor countries were enslaved.

Public meetings take more organising but also have the potential of reaching many more people. You are likely to have a captive audience for an hour or two and can use different ways of keeping people's attention. Videos, speakers from overseas, question and answer sessions, groups work to brainstorm campaign actions, quizzes, food tasting, music and dancing and goods for sale all add variety to an event. If everyone who attends an event takes a simple action such as writing to an MP, it will have a significant impact. As so few people write to their MPs, one letter is taken as representing the concerns of many people (estimates range from ten to one thousand!). Your MP will not be able to ignore your concerns and is likely to agree to a meeting. If you are a constituent of the MP they have an obligation to respond to your letter and concerns.

Joining with the masses

Participating in larger events, whether local or national, can encourage people and help them to see that they are part of a wider movement with a common aim. The mass lobby of the UK Parliament was one such event in June 2002. Martin Gordon, International Campaigns Co-ordinator for Christian Aid, was there:

> Fourteen thousand people travelled hundreds of miles from all over the UK, including groups from schools, universities, churches and trade unions. By 3.00 p.m. we had formed a colourful queue over two miles long, stretching far down the river and over the other side. Over half of the MPs were lobbied by their constituents that day, making it the biggest mass lobby ever in the UK. A variety of trade issues were raised such as a code of conduct for multinational corporations and the need to prevent essential services, like water or education, from being privatised. Campaigners met others from their constituencies and many have co-ordinated follow up visits to their MPs to keep up the pressure. One MP, Hywel Williams,

said, 'it's chaos out there and I can tell you that what you are doing out there is causing a great stir inside this place'.

Contacting decision makers

MPs are often targets for campaign actions, as mentioned for the mass lobby of parliament for trade justice. Tearfund has produced CONNECT!Westminster, a video and book-let with information about how the British government works and ideas on how to contact your local MP and build up a relationship with them. The video includes interviews with Christian MPs from the three main parties, all of whom encourage Christians to engage in the political system so that laws and policies are more influenced by Christian values. CARE has also produced materials called Change Activist, to help Christians engage with the political process at a local, national or European level.

> Sam Moore, a student and Tearfund volunteer in Northern Ireland, started a letter-writing campaign to members of the Northern Ireland Assembly when he discovered they did not use fairly traded tea and coffee. He had a strong case because the Houses of Parlia-ment in London and the Scottish and Welsh Assemblies had already made the switch. He drafted a letter and collected hundreds of signatures from members of his Christian Union. He heard that the Assembly had received many letters but that his was the one that finally forced the issue. Weeks later he was invited to the Assembly to witness the launch of their new fair trade catering policy.

Prayer

When meeting together in groups to discuss issues of in-justice, a natural reaction is to pray about the situation as well as to act by writing letters, signing petitions, joining marches and rallies, etc. Organisations such as Tearfund and SPEAK provide prayer information for their campaigns. Intercessory prayer is closely connected to campaigning in that we are asking the person with power to intervene and bring justice for those who are suffering. In prayer we are asking God to act on behalf of those who are being oppressed or suffering the effects of unjust policies and actions. Including prayer information in any campaigns sheet will help campaigners maintain an ongoing focus on the relevant issues and people affected, and will also be engaging with the powers in the spiritual realms that are behind the earthly reality that we see.

Conclusion

When writing letters, sending postcards, meeting your MP or attending a march, it is good to keep informed about the success of your campaigning. This will encourage you when you see that a company has changed its activities or a government has changed its policies as a result of your actions (e.g. a council switches over to fair trade tea and coffee, the UK government announces more debt relief, an international target to halve those without access to sanitation by 2015 is agreed). It will also help you to know where to target any ongoing campaigning. The environment, development or human rights organisations will be able to keep you updated on the progress of the issues they are working on.

Individuals can make a difference to the lives of those suffering injustice around the world. Over the years campaigning has helped to free people from prison, to persuade companies to stop destructive practices, to cancel unpayable debts and to increase the aid budget. All it takes is for a few concerned people to call for change and those in power need to respond. They know they are being watched and will be held to account. When Christians take a stand against social injustice, God acts in powerful ways. What could happen if you got involved?

Questions for Reflection

- Do you know of any individuals in your church who share you desire to start campaigning for international justice? How can you get together with them?
- Are you aware of any existing campaigning groups in your local area? If so, can you join them?
- Do you receive the campaigns resources from any organisations? If not, which one would be most appropriate for you to contact?
- Which issues of injustice do you feel most passionately about? Do you know of organisations campaigning on these issues? How can you find out more?
- What will be your first step in the next week to do something about this?

Additional Resources

Organisations

Tearfund	< www.tearfund.org >	0845 355 8355
Christian Aid	< www.christian-aid.org >	020 8620 444
CAFOD	< www.cafod.org.uk >	020 7733 7900
SPEAK	< www.speak.org.uk >	020 7249 4309
People and Planet	< www.peopleandplanet.org >	01865 245 678
Amnesty International	< www.amnesty.org.uk >	020 7814 6200
World Development Movement	< www.wdm.org >	0800 328 2153

CARE	< www.changeactivist.org.uk >	020 7233 0455
Movement for Christian Democracy	< www.mcdpolitics.org >	
Friends of the Earth	< www.foe.co.uk >	020 7490 1555

Tearfund Materials

Once a quarter, Tearfund produces *globalaction*, a maga-zine and CD-Rom that provides everything you need to make a difference, including simple campaign actions, prayer points, background information, up-to-date news and PowerPoint presentations. It will keep you in touch and involved with all of Tearfund's campaigns.

CONNECT!Westminster video and booklet (Tearfund, 2001)

For all the latest campaigning news and resources from Tearfund visit: < www.tearfund.org/campaigning > or call 0845 355 8355

For student campaigns see < www.tearfund.org/students >

For Lift the Label, an ethical lifestyle campaign, see <www.tearfund.org/youth >

Materials from other organisations

Change Activist (CARE, 2002)

Act Justly: Six sessions for cells or small groups to help Christians think and act biblically on world issues (London: Christian Aid, 2002)

Groups Manual (SPEAK)

Lattimer, Mark, *The Campaigning Handbook* (London: The Directory of Social Change, 2000)

14

Getting Involved: Bringing Change in Your Local Community

Introduction

Chapter 13 gave some suggestions for how to become a campaigner and add your voice to the proposals for change that others have already initiated, often focused at a national or international level. This chapter offers some tips on how to bring change in your local community and shows how individuals and small groups can bring this about. It concentrates on planning a strategy for influencing those with the power.

Influencing is something that we all do all of the time. If your child has been given a detention at school that you don't think is fair, you may well go and see the teacher to try and persuade him or her to change their mind. If your church leader is proposing to spend all of the church money on a new building that you don't think is appropriate then you are likely to go and speak to him or her and try and persuade them to stop or modify the plans. If you have been sold faulty goods you will go back to the shop and demand your money back or an exchange.

These everyday actions of influencing often try and make life better for those we are closest to, usually friends and family. What this chapter does is to encourage us to broaden the sphere of our influence. First, it broadens it by including those we come across in our neighbourhood who are in some way poor, marginalised or suffering. When Jesus tells the parable of the Good Samaritan he teaches that anyone in need is our neighbour so loving our neighbour as ourselves means loving all of those around us. Secondly, it broadens the issues to consider issues of social justice. This will mean ensuring that our neighbour has basic needs as well as standing up for any injustices that they suffer. Thirdly, it broadens the sphere of influence by suggesting how to influence in a more planned way, so that you will be more effective in bringing the changes to the local community.

Broadening your sphere of influence

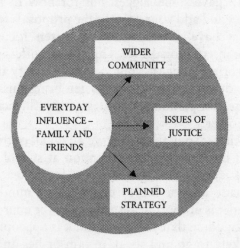

Why Policy Matters

When trying to influence an organisation or individual we are clearly trying to influence their behaviour. Only the desired change in behaviour will bring about the change we want (e.g. the school detention to be cancelled or a refund to be granted for the goods). However, what will usually determine the behaviour of the organisation or individual is their policy behind the relevant matter. So we may need to influence policies in order to influence behaviour.

These policies come in many forms. For example:

* Unwritten rules about the way things are done (e.g. a teacher or school that gives detentions to the whole class if one pupil misbehaves).
* A written document produced by the organisation (e.g. a shop that offers a refund if the goods are faulty and a receipt is provided).
* A government law that organisations have to implement (e.g. the local authority needing to provide housing for those who are homeless, or a bank needing to limit the rate of interest they can charge on a loan).

Planning for Change

The rest of the chapter uses an example from Bradford, UK. It shows how one church, aiming to reduce solvent abuse in its local area, managed to get a national law changed, to influence the local curriculum in schools, and to educate local children about the issues. It is an overview of how to plan for change and is based on Tearfund's 'Advocacy Cycle', which is shown below. More details of planning to influence decision makes can be found in Tearfund's Advocacy Toolkit.[1]

Background

In 1997 Chantelle Bleau died, aged sixteen, from the inhalation of butane gas. Soon after her death Chantelle's parents, Pat and Richard Bleau, along with Paul Scanlon, Senior Pastor of the Abundant Life Church, where they are members, founded the Chantelle Bleau Memorial Fund (CBMF). Its initial aim was to raise awareness of the dangers of volatile

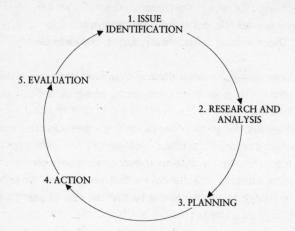

substance abuse (VSA), in particular butane gas lighter fuel. It was set up as part of the Abundant Life Church and became an independent charity in 2001, although it is still closely connected with the church.

STEP 1: Identify the issue
The first step in any plan to bring about change is to identify the issue you are trying to address.

Chantelle's death could have been avoided. She was anti-drugs and had even appeared in an anti-drugs play two weeks prior to her death. Although she was aware that inhalation of lighter fuel was something she should not have been doing, she was unaware of the potential danger she was placing herself in. Her parents and others at their church concluded that young people were generally unaware of the dangers of lighter fuel and other volatile solvents (such as aerosols, glues and fire extinguishers) and that education about these dangers could prevent such deaths in the future. That was the main reason for setting up the fund.

STEP 2: Undertake research
The second step is to find out more of the facts so that you
will be able to develop clear proposals for change.

CBMF undertook some research to find out the exact details
of VSA. The St George's Hospital Medical School in Liver-
pool had data on VSA since 1971 and this showed that it was
responsible for more deaths in people under eighteen than
any other drug, including heroine, ecstasy and cocaine, even
though its use was much lower than these drugs. Figures
showed that lighter fuel was responsible for over half of
these deaths, roughly thirty per year in the past ten years.
The Medical School had also been undergoing their own
campaign since the mid-1990s trying to raise awareness of
the issues, so the staff welcomed the increased interest.

CBMF also contacted Re-Solv, a national drugs charity
that raises awareness and gives advice on VSA. Re-Solv
gave useful information on the national situation and both
organisations shared resources and discussed different
approaches together.

Their research highlighted that the laws against buying
lighter fuel over the counter were weak and poorly enforced.
The law prohibited shopkeepers from selling lighter fuel to
under-sixteens if 'they knew the gas was for purposes of
abuse'. In effect, they rarely refused sales meaning that
lighter fuel was more readily accessible than cigarettes to
those under sixteen. This discovery led the staff at CBMF to
think about taking their campaign wider than just education
and to investigate possibilities about tightening up the
national law, particularly with regard to lighter fuel.

STEP 3: Action planning
The third step is to plan exactly how you will bring about
the change you want. It involves developing clear proposals
for what you want to happen, building alliances with those

who are sympathetic and identifying those with the power to implement your proposals.

Developing proposals. As a result of the research, CBMF decided that they needed to take a twin-track approach. They recognised that most change was going to come about through education and raising awareness in schools and the local community so that people would be aware of the dangers of lighter fuel and would stop buying it, i.e. to prevent the demand. For this they needed to develop education materials and gain access to schools and youth clubs. However, they also wanted to change the law so that it became illegal to sell lighter fuel to young people under eighteen, i.e. to prevent the supply. They therefore had positive alternatives to the law and a clear message to bring to children in the schools.

Building alliances. As well as the specialist organisations dealing with solvent abuse, CBMF approached youth clubs and schools, which are the main groups in frequent contact with the young people who were most at risk from solvent abuse. Having a good relationship with the schools and other local groups has been vital to the success of their work, both in education and in influencing what is included in the drugs education curriculum of the Local Education Authority. They also approached local councillors and the national drugs tsar to encourage them to join in the effort to change the law. However, it wasn't easy at the start and some of these groups needed a lot of convincing. Some of the strongest allies can actually be antagonistic at the start so perseverance is necessary. As Christian Allsworth, the first full-time staff member of the foundation, explains:

> Initially, the reaction from many local people was disbelief. They didn't believe that solvent abuse was such a problem,

thinking that maybe one or two people each year died from it. However, once we showed them the facts, they were willing to listen. We now have good contacts with youth organisations and regularly give talks to them. We have access to thirty-six schools in Bradford and have maybe made inroads into twenty of them. Our experience and local focus gives us credibility and the young people relate well to us.

Identifying those with power to bring change. Staff at CBMF quickly identified the head teachers of the secondary schools and the youth workers throughout the city as those who could give them access to the young people in order to educate them about the dangers of solvent abuse. The head teacher usually determined the assemblies but the teachers responsible for social education determined what would be taught on social issues such as drug abuse. Therefore, CBMF not only needed permission from the head teacher to get access to the schools, they also had to work with the teachers responsible for social education to determine what they could teach during the lessons.

Secondly, because the law is determined at a national level they needed to influence the national parliament. The obvious step was to contact their local MP to discuss how he could help them bring about the changes they desired and how he could use his influence as an MP. For proposals like theirs, which are not part of the main government programme of legislation, individual MPs can initiate legislation and support its passage through Parliament.

The third area they focused on was influencing the curriculum in local schools. There is a national initiative called the Healthy Schools Strategy and, as part of this, each Local Education Authority needs to teach children about the dangers of drug abuse. CBMF therefore made contact with the person responsible for this, and were present at the discussions when they set the curriculum.

STEP 4: Action
This involves speaking directly with those you want to
influence. In practice, step 3 and step 4 overlap because you
are likely to try and influence those with power from the
time that you first meet them.

Engage with those who can bring about policy change.
Gerry Sutcliffe, the local MP, was sympathetic to their proposals of changing the law and he invited representatives
from CBMF to go to the House of Commons to address a
group of MPs. Five of these, led by Gerry, joined a parliamentary group on solvent abuse. They drafted legislation to
govern the sales of butane lighter fuels and CBMF, as well
as other agencies, such as Re-Solv, worked with this parliamentary group over the following months. They provided
briefings and summaries of the scale of the problem. There
was also a debate held in the House of Commons and the
Department for Trade and Industry initiated a nationwide
consultation. This resulted in legislation being passed in
October 1999 that made it illegal to sell butane gas lighter
fuel to under-eighteens.

Christian Allsworth also maintained links with the Local
Education Authority, saying:

> I work closely with the woman in charge of the Healthy
> Schools Strategy for the Local Education Authority. We plan
> together what information about solvent misuse should be
> shared with children at each stage in the curriculum to ensure
> that they are well informed about the dangers, but not too
> swamped with facts.

Make the most of any change in policy. Once a law or
policy has been changed, it is vital to make sure that it is
implemented; otherwise its purpose is limited. It is also
good to be ready to take advantage of any unexpected

spin-offs from the policy work. This particular change in the law has had various positive effects. One is that solvent abuse will be an essential part of the national curriculum citizenship course in schools from 2004. Previously, it was only optional, whereas teaching on Class A drugs (such as cocaine), tobacco and alcohol was obligatory. This recognises the increasing understanding of the dangers of solvent abuse, partly attributed to the issues raised in the parliamentary debate when the bill was being passed. CBMF now receive more interest from schools that want them to come in and teach these specific lessons. According to Christian, the change in law has also been a useful backup to their education work:

> When we go into schools, we focus primarily on prevention through education. However, we use the existence of the law to back up our case, explaining that it is not there to spoil people's fun, but to protect them. It acts as an extra string to our bow. Having the limit at eighteen is helpful as it covers almost everyone of school age.

However, although the law has been changed, it is not being enforced as rigorously as it could be. In neighbouring county of Derbyshire, the police use young people to undertake 'test purchases' where they will go into shops to try and buy lighter fuel without proof of age. If they are able to do it, the shopkeeper will receive a warning and repeated breach of the law will result in a fine, and could even lead to imprisonment or temporary suspension of the right to trade. However, in Bradford this isn't happening and most of the shops will still sell indiscriminately. Christian says:

> I know the police are busy with other things but I would like to see test purchasing in Bradford, to raise awareness among the shopkeepers and to cut down the supply. At CBMF we have

good relations with the police and I am encouraging them to tighten up the implementation of this law. If it is happening in other areas, why can't it happen here?

STEP 5: Evaluate your success
The last step is to evaluate the results of your work and to decide if you need to change your approach, keep going or stop because you have achieved all you wanted.

The latest report into VSA shows a drop in the deaths in 2000, the first full year after the legislation came into play. St George's Hospital Medical School say, 'The decrease in deaths in 2000 is primarily due to a reduction in deaths associated with abuse of butane lighter refills by people under the age of eighteen.' They welcome this reduction, but recognise that it is too early to attribute this directly to the change in law. However, if it is due to the change in law, then this law needs to be properly implemented. Encouraging the local police to enforce it therefore becomes crucial.

CBMF still focus their work on education. Christian says that one of the reasons for their success is that they have not relied solely on changing the law to bring about their desired change in people, but have used the law as a tool to back up their local education work. It has reinforced what they are doing and made the work in schools more effective. However, a change in the law has not replaced the need for strong relationships at local level and education work to bring about behaviour change. In fact, CBMF are just about to launch a peer education programme to train up those in the last year of school (either seventeen- and eighteen-year-olds) to be role models to younger children to help prevent them getting into solvent abuse.

Conclusion

A small, dedicated group of Christians have been able to protect children in their local communities from the dangers of solvent abuse. They have done this through education, through building good links with local groups and through changing national legislation. Members of the church, in their spare time, have provided the main impetus for change and have provided a strong support role for each other. This is just one example of a church at the centre of bringing good news to its local community and being faithful to its mission. What could happen if you got involved?

Questions for Reflection

For the problem you are trying to address, go through each of the steps above:

- What is the problem and what are its causes?
- Who can you work with to have a better chance of achieving success, both locally and nationally?
- Who are the main targets, i.e. those with the power to bring about change?
- What solutions are you proposing to solve the problem?
- What methods will you use to bring about change?
- How will you know if you have been successful?

15

Christian Distinctiveness: Vision, Values and Policymaking

Introduction

This chapter considers some of the more fundamental questions that should form the basis of a Christian approach to involvement in issues of social justice. What kind of society do we want? What values should underpin our involvement? How can we engage in policymaking? It is based on biblical truth. The context is God bringing about his kingdom and using the church to do so. We are called not just to work for change, but also to do so in a way that will bring glory to God, maintaining our values and integrity of character.

Developing a Vision for Change

It is vital to have an idea of what the world could be like and what we are trying to do before we engage in any activity that is involved in transforming society. We need a vision for change, which is a dream of how the world could be or how we want the world to be. It will answer the question, 'What could happen if we got involved?'

When Jesus speaks in the synagogue in Nazareth, he refers to Isaiah's vision of the coming of the kingdom of God, which has already come in part and awaits its final fulfilment:

> The Spirit of the LORD is on me, because he has anointed me to preach good news to the poor. He has sent me to proclaim freedom for the prisoners and recovery of sight for the blind, to release the oppressed, to proclaim the year of the LORD's favour (Lk. 4:18–19).

The vision that Christians have is the fullness of salvation, in other words, putting things right and reversing the effects of sin, bringing healing at all levels: spiritual, physical, emotional, individual, societal and political. It is the restoration of the earth and its people to the glory and joy that God intended from the beginning. It is something that God has already started and we are given glimpses in the prophets of the final state (Isa. 11:1–9, 25:1–8, 65:17–25).

This future hope is not just wishful thinking, but is based on God's promises and on the fact that God already has victory over Satan and all the evil powers of this world (Col. 2:15; 1 Pet. 3:22). Any actions we undertake to bring about change are therefore based on the understanding of who has already won, and motivated by the hope that comes from the faith in an all-powerful God.

FAITH $\longrightarrow$ HOPE $\longrightarrow$ ACTION $\longrightarrow$ CHANGE

Amongst all the suffering and injustice, this hope can give us the strength to carry on, knowing both that a better future lies ahead and that God hates injustice. We are motivated by love and compassion, not anger. We look forward to justice, not backwards to revenge. We also need to remember that any work we do is God's work in which he allows us to participate. He is therefore ultimately responsible for change.

A vision also needs to be tempered with a healthy dose of realism. We should have an awareness of what we can change and focus on that, as opposed to choosing issues that will just wear us out without producing any change.

A vision for social change for our society considers what the kingdom of God will look like in our own context, what the characteristics of the good news will be in our village, city or country. This could include everyone having access to clean water, a community without violence or tension, everyone having the chance to know God, leaders serving the people and being accountable to them.

One of the best-known and most inspiring visions about the kind of country he wanted was given by Martin Luther King Jr at the march on Washington for jobs and freedom.[1]

I have a dream that one day this nation will rise up and live out the true meaning of its creed: 'We hold these truths to be self-evident: that all men are created equal.' I have a dream that one day on the red hills of Georgia the sons of former slaves and the sons of former slave-owners will be able to sit down together at a table of brotherhood. I have a dream that one day even the state of Mississippi, a desert state, sweltering with the heat of injustice and oppression, will be transformed into an oasis of freedom and justice. I have a dream that my four children will one day live in a nation where they will not be judged by the colour of their skin but by the content of their character. I have a dream today.

I have a dream that one day the state of Alabama, whose governor's lips are presently dripping with the words of interposition and nullification, will be transformed into a situation where little black boys and black girls will be able to join hands with little white boys and white girls and walk together as sisters and brothers. I have a dream today. I have a dream that one day every valley shall be exalted, every hill and mountain shall be made low, the rough places will be made plain, and the crooked places will be made straight, and the glory of the LORD shall be revealed, and all flesh shall see it together. This is our hope. This is the faith with which I return to the South. With this faith we will be able to hew out of the mountain of despair a stone of hope. With this faith we will be able to transform the jangling discords of our nation into a beautiful symphony of brother-hood. With this faith we will be able to work together, to pray together, to struggle together, to go to jail together, to stand up for freedom together, knowing that we will be free one day …

When we let freedom ring, when we let it ring from every village and every hamlet, from every state and every city, we will be able to speed up that day when all of God's children, black men and white men, Jews and Gentiles, Protestants and Catholics, will be able to join hands and sing in the words of the old Negro spiritual, 'Free at last! Free at last! Thank God Almighty, we are free at last!'

Maintaining Christian Values

Before engaging, we also need to know what we stand for; in other words, we must identify the values or principles that we want to see at the heart of any society. These will also form the basis of the values that we follow ourselves as we seek to live lives consistent with what we are asking others to do. A comprehensive list of these principles would be very extensive so below are some of the key principles and underlying ethics in the Old Testament that Jesus affirmed in his ministry. These therefore form the basis of the values that would underpin our work and that we would seek to have at the heart of any society.

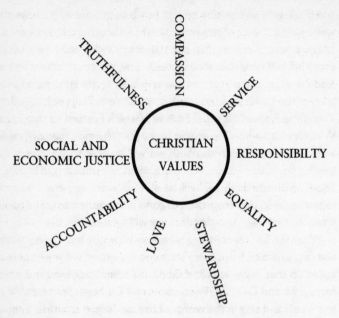

Compassion

The psalmist speaks of God being 'compassionate and gracious' who is 'slow to anger and abounding in love' (Ps. 86:15). We are required to be the same and are promised the Holy Spirit to help us. As Wieland claims:

> We could say that an indicator, an irrefutable testimony of our being full of the Holy Spirit is the capacity to allow ourselves to be moved to compassion when we are faced with the weak or with those whose rights have been denied or who are ignored and excluded by society.[2]

However, this compassion will not come about in a vacuum. We need to get to know people who are suffering injustice or poverty, to understand their situation. In other words, we need to get involved. When injustice is treated at a global level we often become angry about what we see, but only when we see those who are suffering as individuals with names, families, skills and dreams are we moved to compassion, like the Good Samaritan. If we stand on the sidelines and observe from afar, our compassion will be measured and our response tempered. However, when we rejoice with those who are rejoicing and mourn with those who are mourning then we will take on other people's struggles as our own and get involved.

Developing a Godly Character

God requires justice in all aspects of our lives, not just in the public sphere. He demands righteous hearts as well as social justice. He wants justice in the family and the community as well as in the courts. Therefore, as Christians involved in fighting for justice, our own personal lives need to reflect the values that we are fighting for. For many leaders, personal morality is seen as irrelevant to public office. However, as Christians, we cannot separate them. If injustice is due to the breakdown of relationships at all levels, then we need to work to restore relationships at all levels, from family to national and international. We need to model the kind of world we want to live in, and the kind of behaviour we expect from our leaders.

However, even when speaking up for these values, we will often face the struggle to be true to them ourselves. That is why it is essential to jealously guard our time with God. It is a temptation for activists to be too busy for reflection. But this reflection is necessary in order to understand what is happening in our situation and to receive strength and guidance from God. Paul instructs us to pray at all times and we are told to put on the full armour of God. Jesus frequently spent time alone in order to give him the strength and understanding to carry out his mission. If we do not protect our inner life, we are unlikely to be able to listen to God effectively or to respond to what he is doing and what he asks us to join in with.

Service

We need to get our hands dirty. We need to become involved by serving. Our attitude should be the same as that of Jesus:

> Who, being in very nature God,
> did not consider equality with God something to be grasped,
> but made himself nothing,
> taking the very nature of a servant,
> being made in human likeness.
> And being found in appearance as a man,
> he humbled himself
> and became obedient to death – even death on a cross!
>
> (Phil. 2:6–8)

He emptied himself of power in order to serve people. We do not approach people with all of the answers. Rather, we should approach them with a willingness to work with them to overcome the oppression or injustice that they face.

Social and economic justice

Many of the laws in Leviticus were written to promote justice, such as using fair measurements for trade (Lev. 19:36), not charging interest (Lev. 25:36), fair distribution of land (Lev. 25:8–54) and paying fair wages to labourers (Mal. 3:5). As seen earlier, Jesus uses his mission statement to identify his reign with the Year of Jubilee and the bringing of justice to all relationships and all aspects of society. He rebukes the Pharisees for their neglect of justice (Mt. 23:23). This has been outlined in detail in chapter 3.

Love

Jesus placed love at the heart of all commandments (Mt. 22:37–40) and says that we will be judged according to how we treat others (Mt. 25:31–46). This means that we are to love everyone, the rich and the poor, the oppressor and the oppressed. We are to respond to hatred with love:

> Love your enemies and pray for those who persecute you … If you love those who love you, what reward will you get … and if you greet only your brothers, what are you doing more than others … be perfect, therefore, as your heavenly Father is perfect (Mt. 5:46–48).

Reconciliation

This love therefore opens up a way to reconciliation between the perpetrators of injustice and those who are suffering, between the poor who are being exploited and those who are profiting. As Martin Luther King Jr said, 'Non-cooperation and boycotts are not ends in themselves; they are merely means to awaken a sense of moral shame in the opponent. The end is redemption and reconciliation.'[3]

Wise stewardship of resources

Human beings have been given responsibility for looking after creation in the way that God wants (Gen. 1–2). This means treating the environment with respect, taking proper care of all animals, fish and birds, and using the earth's natural resources to the benefit of all people, not just a few. This has implications for how we use our resources for the current generation (e.g. ensuring that people have access to land so that they can grow their own food; preventing operations by factories that pollute local water sources or destroy the environment; and ensuring that when animals are reared for food they are done so in a humane way). It also has implications for future generations, as we need to ensure that the earth will be able to support them in years to come. This means reducing pollution that contributes to global warming; maintaining forests and other areas of land that are essential for growing food; and, ultimately, reducing our consumption to sustainable levels. Again, we need to be consistent in our own lives, e.g. cutting down air travel and increasing recycling, so that we implement what we ask others to do.

Equality

All human beings are equal before God, regardless of age, gender, race, or intelligence because all human beings are made in his image (Gen. 1–2). No one should be discriminated against and everyone should have access to services like healthcare and education, and to jobs and housing. This should be based on need, and not privilege. In our individual relationships, especially with those who are poor or victims of injustice, it is important that we recognise them as equals, with talents and skills, who are able to contribute to liberating themselves from the situation they are in.

Individual responsibility

There is also responsibility for each person to use the gifts and talents they have been given to the best of their abilities (Mt. 25:14–30). Therefore, any laws and policies should allow for this freedom and responsibility for people to use what they have been given by God, within the limits of responsibility towards others (e.g. a system of social welfare should support those who have no other means of work, but, at the same time, there should be encouragement to work for those who can).

Truthfulness

It is a well-known saying that 'power corrupts and absolute power corrupts absolutely'. One of the first things to be compromised when people have access to power is truthfulness. When engaging with those in power, we need to speak the truth at all times and to communicate it in such a way that others understand it and accept it. If we believe that what we are saying is right, then we can show the evidence and make a clear case for change. If we distort the facts then not only are we being dishonest, but we may be arguing for a change that will not bring the desired benefits.

Accountability

Decisions are taken in secret and those in power often hide the truth or present facts in a misleading way. We need to hold those in power to account for their actions and to ensure that what they do is in the open so that everyone can see. Not only will this help more people to participate in decisions that will affect their lives, but it will also ensure that actions by companies and governments are done for the benefit to the population as a whole. Fewer dishonest or destructive actions are taken if people know they have to be accountable for them.

Knowing the values that we stand for will help us to engage in influencing those in power on the basis of our Christian character and will also help us to know which values or principles we think should form the basis of actions by those in power. One way of influencing decision makers is through policymaking, so we need to understand how we can apply biblical values to policymaking.

Engaging in the Policy Debate

Most of us live in a pluralistic society, where there are many competing interests from different groups. From a Christian perspective, we know God's plan for humanity and we know the principles by which he would like his people to live. We need to engage with the policy makers to ensure our concerns are heard, but also to recognise that we live in a democracy.

Before engaging in any policymaking we need to understand that 'compromise' will be involved, i.e. that any laws or policies are unlikely to be exactly as we want them to be. Biblical principles are pure and are reflections of God's character. The state and the laws it enacts are God's instruments to help bring about his kingdom, but the state is fallen and will never be able to produce laws that are a perfect reflection of God's laws. Compromise is also inevitable because we do not live in a Christian state. The laws will therefore be produced through democratic discussion and agreement.

When contributing to practical law making and policymaking, we cannot just present policies and support them by claiming, 'this is what it says in the Bible' unless the majority in that country see biblical principles as a valid basis for policymaking. We will need to couch it in language that others understand and would agree with, and apply them to the modern context. In other words, we need to *contextualise* biblical values into policies. This involves taking truths or principles from the Bible, without necessarily identifying the ultimate origin of those ideas. We can talk about the responsibility of humans to one another without saying that this responsibility is ultimately to God. We can talk about the inherent value of human beings, without saying that that value comes from being made in God's image. We can talk about the necessity of justice without saying that this is based on God's character.

Applying Biblical Values to Policymaking
There is not the space to treat this theme in detail. However, below are a few key points on the Bible and policymaking, These are expanded in great detail in many books on Christian ethics.[4]

- The Bible is God's source of truth but not every kind of truth for every situation.
- Jesus' approach to the law should guide our approach. Whatever he affirms as continuing from the Old Testament is clearly relevant for the church and the world today.
- The Bible provides moral guidance in different ways. [5]
- There are different types of law in the Old Testament, some of which still apply today and others that do not.
- The law has a limited role and cannot bring righteousness.
- The law was given to a different society at different times.
- God progressively reveals himself throughout the Old Testament and no laws can be considered as a full revelation.

It is a way of participating in the debate in a language that others understand but without compromising our own principles. It relies on developing a Christian mindset so that we are confident that we are being faithful to God's truth, even if we are not directly quoting from the Bible. We do not deny the origin of our principles nor do we try and deceive others; the aim is to ensure that our proposals make sense to those who have different beliefs and values. *Contextualisation* promotes policy ideas on pragmatic grounds and wins arguments by showing that the proposals are best for everyone involved (e.g. through preventing family breakdown, encouraging employment, rebuilding communities, as shown in the example of the Elim church in Cambourne in chapter 2). This is particularly important in a democracy. It is possible to reach substantial agreement with others on many issues (e.g. the injustice of continuing debt burden) but the difference often lies in the justification for the position taken.

> Tearfund has been lobbying in the UK on issues of international trade. Many of the views or positions developed are the same as those of key non-Christian NGOs working on the issue but Tearfund was careful not to just blindly follow the consensus approach but to develop principles from the Bible. Biblical principles regarding trade include the facts that (a) governments have responsibility for the welfare of their people (Rom. 13); (b) we are stewards of the world with the responsibility to look after it (Gen. 1:28); (c) everyone is made in God's image and worthy or respect (Gen. 1:27); (d) human beings are created to work and to be creative (Gen. 1:28); and (e) resources are to be used for the benefit of all people and not for the few (Lev. 25).
>
> The implications of this in policymaking are that (a) governments should be able to put certain conditions on businesses (e.g. to employ local people or use local materials, so that the people in that country benefit from the business). There should be limitations to what is left to market forces (e.g. essential services such as health and education, so that the government can ensure that people's basic needs are met); (b) business should behave in an environmentally responsible way, reducing pollution and overall environmental impact; (c) workers should be treated with respect and be given a wage that they can live on and able to work in decent conditions; (d) businesses should seek ways of creating and keeping jobs, and governments should work with them to do this – full employment should be a goal of any government.

However, a *contextualisation* strategy is only a partial response. It cannot communicate the transcendent aspects of a biblical vision for human living. It can only make a muted challenge to idolatry, pointing out false gods but not necessarily pointing to the one true God. In this way, it can be seen as a necessary compromise that is not the ideal we want but is realistic in a fallen world and only one part of a response by the church. If the church's contribution to the policy debate were all through a method of *contextualising* biblical values into secular language and concepts, the church would not be faithful to its calling of proclaiming truth, offering hope and working for change. The public arena would also miss an important contribution, as it needs to be reminded of the transcendent.

As outlined in chapters 2–4, the church therefore needs to engage in the public arena in many different ways. It needs to speak out prophetically, clearly stating God's truth from the Bible and recognising that Christianity provides the only adequate account of reality. It needs to engage in prayer, recognising that policy change is part of the spiritual battle. It needs to consider civil disobedience if the law of the land is unjust and clearly against God's law and there is no other way of trying to bring about change. It also needs to lead by example, showing that living by certain biblical values brings benefits to society. Finally, the church needs to be true to its overall mission of preaching the good news, caring for the needy and contributing to social development.

Questions for Reflection

- What is your vision for what you want your community, region or country to be like in five, ten or twenty years' time? What role do you think the church can have?
- What would you say are the most important values you want to see underpinning your society?
- How would you answer someone who says any Christian involvement in law making or policymaking inevitably leads to compromise? How can you avoid this compromise?

- How would you formulate a biblical perspective on issues such as divorce, social security, or asylum? How would you contextualise these into the law of your country?

Further Reading

Bauckham, R., *The Bible in Politics: How to Read the Bible Politically*

Cook, David, *The Moral Maze: A Way of Exploring Christian Ethics*

Hays, Richard B., *The Moral Vision of the New Testament: A Contemporary Introduction to New Testament Ethics*

Mott, Stephen, *Biblical Ethics and Social Change*

Schluter, Michael (ed.), *Christianity in a Changing World: Biblical Insight on Contemporary Issues*

Stott, John, *New Issues Facing Christians Today*

Swartley, Willard M., *Slavery, Sabbath, War and Women: Case Issues in Biblical Interpretation*

Townsend, C and J. Ashcroft, *Political Christians in a Plural Society*

Wright, Chris J.H., *Living as the People of God: The Relevance of Old Testament Ethics*

Wright, Chris J.H., *Walking in the Ways of the Lord: The Ethical Authority of the Old Testament*

Difficult Issues: Civil Disobedience and Human Rights

Introduction

Whether to engage in civil disobedience and what to make of the human rights agenda are two issues that have caused problems for Christians. With civil disobedience the question is often 'what can Christians be involved in?' or 'how far can Christians go?' With human rights the concern is often that Christians will be involved in developing laws and policies that are based on secular concepts. This chapter seeks to explore these issues and to offer some suggestions for the way forward.

Issue 1: Civil Disobedience

It was mentioned in chapter 4 that, in certain circumstances, civil disobedience could be an option open to the church when engaging with power. But how far can we go? When can disobeying the government be legitimate from a biblical standpoint? Before we can answer such questions, we need to understand what civil disobedience means.

Civil disobedience is when people deliberately disobey rules or laws as a way of trying to bring about change or showing dissatisfaction with the current situation. Prosecution happens through government courts because governments are the only ones who can make laws. It is therefore useful to consider civil disobedience as breaking the rules or laws of the government, even if they are not the main targets of the action (e.g. breaking into a weapons factory will result in arrest by the police and prosecution by the government even if the main focus of the protest is against the company manufacturing the weapons).

Most civil disobedience seeks to act within the current system, thus recognising the validity of the system, if not all of its actions (e.g. the bus boycott led by Marin Luther King Jr to seek the end of segregation through changing the law. People avoided using the buses as an act of civil disobedience, but the actions were directed towards the authorities, which they depended upon to bring about change.) However, some civil disobedience does not recognise the validity of the system and seeks to overthrow it, such as the people power movement in the Philippines that peacefully overthrew Marcos in 1986 and the non-violent revolution in East Germany that was instrumental in bringing down the Berlin Wall.

However, no activity that constitutes violence against people or is part of a violent revolution that seeks to overthrow the existing rulers is considered here as civil disobedience. Certain groups would consider violent actions as part of civil disobedience, such as some anarchist groups that see fighting the police as part of their actions to undermine the present system. However, violence is not an option open to Christians. It can therefore be helpful to talk about *non-violent civil disobedience* or *non-violent direct action*.

Any activities that are lawful do not constitute civil disobedience. They can be seen as constructive engagement with the powers and part of the conventional range of methods available to bring about justice. These include strikes (if they are legal in the country), boycotts, public marches and rallies, meetings, visiting members of parliament, awareness-raising campaigns and media stunts. Some of these activities, such as strikes and boycotts, target companies and governments hoping to cause damage to their profits or reputation, but still operating within the limits of the law. Some are symbolic actions that aim to highlight injustices. These may include actions such as holding a silent vigil for those who have 'disappeared' as was popular in Argentina by women seeking to find their missing husbands, or staging a media stunt outside an arms fair. Symbolic actions are a powerful and important part of campaigning.

Because civil disobedience is a last resort, any decision to become involved needs to be considered seriously. Below are some possible criteria to think about before involvement:

- The law opposed is immoral.
- Every possible non-disobedient option has been exhausted.
- God's will has been sought and all objections have been adequately addressed.
- The action is not excessive.
- There is no violence against people.
- The action is public and aiming to find a solution.
- There is likelihood of success.
- There is awareness of what the penalty is, and of potential repercussions, and a willingness to accept these, such as arrest and imprisonment.
- Actions are in line with Christian character.

Consideration of Violence

As mentioned earlier, violence is not an option to be considered. Much has been written on this[1] and there is not space to go through all of the arguments, so a few theological and practical considerations are offered below:

Theological Considerations	Practical Considerations
Jesus prohibited the use of force in bringing about his kingdom (Mt. 26:50–56) and instead chose to model servant leadership. He brought about change through suffering and through challenging the authorities. Christians are called to be peacemakers and peace is at the heart of God's mission (Mt. 5:7). We are called to love our enemies and pray for those who persecute us (Mt. 5:44). Murder is forbidden and hatred of others will be judged by God (Mt. 5:21–22). We are instructed by God not to take revenge (Mt. 5:38–42). God says he will avenge (Rom. 12:19) and that we need to overcome evil by good. Immediately after this Paul talks about the role of the state in punishing evil (Rom. 13:3–4). God's authority is higher than the state's (Col. 1:16). We are to be motivated by love in all we do (1 Cor. 13; Col. 3:14).	Using violence is no guarantee that the situation will be any better after you have achieved what you aim to do – it may cause more suffering and injustice in the process than would have been caused otherwise. Violence is often conducted on behalf of others (terrorist groups, violent revolutionaries) with little consultation with the people they are claiming to represent. If a new group comes to power through violent actions, they may simply replace an old oppressive regime with a new one, claiming to speak for the people but not allowing the people to participate in decision-making. Violence dehumanises the person who is doing it and reduces them to the level of the oppressor. By doing this, the oppressor has, in one respect, won, as their morals have dictated the course of action. Those who are fighting for justice have right on their side, and this should not be compromised by actions that simply emulate the oppressors and perpetrators of injustice.

Examples of Civil Disobedience

Direct action

Direct action is the most basic form of civil disobedience and it involves specifically targeted actions that flout the law to show that it is wrong, or make a point about immoral or unjust behaviour when this seems to be the only way left to try and change the situation. In many ways it constitutes non-cooperation with the system with the aim of changing it. It could include obstructing a right of way, non-payment of taxes to the government, organising a political meeting or publishing literature where this is banned, or becoming a conscientious objector to a war and facing imprisonment, as many Americans did during the Vietnam War, including world champion boxer Muhammad Ali.

In early 2003 non-violent direct action was increasing in the UK because, even after one million people marched to protest against any war in Iraq, protesters felt as though their voices were not being heard and had no other option but to revert to direct action such as obstructing military bases and public highways.

> **Martin Luther King and the US Civil Rights Movement**
>
> Direct action was central to the US civil rights campaign. Martin Luther King was relentless in trying to persuade the authorities to change laws and bring equality for all citizens. He also upheld the right to disobey unjust laws, while continually stressing that non-violent resistance was the most potent weapon available to oppressed people. This was because resistance brought on a crisis and forced the community and those in power to face an issue they had hitherto failed to confront. It was a last option when nothing else seemed to be working.
>
> Protests included sit-ins, marches and boycotts. In Alabama they boycotted the buses for over a year. This action was declared illegal by the authorities, with the ringleaders tried by the courts and

convicted for their involvement. There were sit-ins by black college students protesting at segregation in student canteens across the southern United States. This was effectively trespassing in an area (part of the university canteen) that the law denied them access to. King was also heavily involved in legal forms of protest such as the 200,000-strong march on Washington in 1963 to demand equal justice for all citizens under the law, when he delivered his famous 'I have a dream' speech.

Damage of property (non-violent)

Damaging property is another form of civil disobedience and activities could include puncturing an oil pipeline if the drilling company is engaged in human rights abuses (although you need to consider the environmental consequences), damaging weapons of mass destruction if it is clear that they will be used for oppression or breaking through a gate to trespass on private property. The 'non-violent' nature of this action means there is no violence against people, and a commitment not to hurt people. Activities will be carefully planned to cause strategic damage to property to make a point. It will not lead to wanton destruction and will mean that any anger against injustice will be carefully channelled and not allowed to explode into random acts of violence against property or people. It will inevitably mean a willingness to be arrested and be subject to the legal punishment for the actions. Being prepared to suffer the consequences of an action shows respect for the law while drawing attention to the injustice of certain laws or other unjust actions.

Non-violent damage to property does not allow the types of activities that have become increasingly popular in recent years in Europe for a small element of protesters, such as going on a march against the effects of globalisation and smashing in shops, businesses and other establishments seen to represent the face of globalisation.

There are three key differences between violent and non-violent damage to property. First, people involved in violent actions consider violence against people as an option if they are prevented from doing what they have set out to do. For example, if police or security prevents them from trespassing, they would consider using force to continue their activities. Hence, they are not willing to give themselves over to arrest and suffer the consequences of their actions. Secondly, this form of action is less controlled and the anger against injustice may be closer to hatred, especially if there are no positive alternatives that they are proposing. It therefore does not allow agreement to be made between those in power and those with the grievance and does not offer the possibility of reconciliation, which has always to be the ultimate aim of engagement. Thirdly, as a result of less-controlled anger, this action may lead to indiscriminate damage and violence that is way beyond what was needed to make a point.

Non-violent revolution
A non-violent revolution can occur when the sheer weight of numbers publicly demanding a change overcome the system through non-violent means. However, it is an option that is likely to be used infrequently! It is much more dependent on the circumstances in the country and whether there is a groundswell of opinion that wants the existing regime to be replaced through non-violent means, and whether the leaders are determined to steer a course of non-violence. However, it is worth mentioning because these non-violent revolutions have brought change in the Philippines (twice) and in Eastern Europe.

Marcos was president of the Philippines from 1965 until 1986. During this time he abolished Congress and declared martial law. In 1983 former opposition Senator Aquino was killed by the Marcos regime and two million people came to the funeral, shocked at what happened and afraid that it could happen to them. Following this, there was pressure for elections and Marcos called snap elections for February 1986. Contrary to all evidence he declared himself the winner against Mrs. Aquino, widow of the former senator. Those in charge of counting votes walked out, complaining that they had been pressurised to falsify data. Those monitoring the elections declared that the result had been fixed.

Soon afterwards some key army officials, led by Fidel Ramos, defected from the Marcos government and holed themselves up in their barracks. Marcos sent in the army to fight them, raising the prospect of a bloody battle. The leading Roman Catholic Cardinal called on the radio for people to form a human buffer around the troops that had defected, in order to prevent bloodshed. The Christian research organisation ISACC also issued a call to the Protestants to join and thousands of people flocked from all over the country.

For four days and nights people stayed there, with numbers swelling each day. Meanwhile both Marcos and Aquino had independently sworn themselves in as President. The tanks did not break through the human buffer and gradually more key army leaders defected to join Ramos, until the balance of power had swung in his favour, meaning that Marcos could not remain in power. The streets erupted in celebrations as the people realised they had used non-violent means to overthrow the seemingly immovable political powers. Marcos fled the country and Aquino became the new President, resulting in a re-establishment of formal political democracy and participation.

Issue 2: The Human Rights Approach

The concept of human rights often causes problems for Christians. Some Christians maintain that we have no rights (we have been saved by grace) so we cannot talk of human rights. Others say that human rights are a secular concept. Christians should therefore steer well clear of them. Still others are reacting to the prevailing individualistic interpretation of human rights, without any ensuing responsibility, where people will demand their own rights without considering their obligation to provide for the rights of others.

Whatever Christians do, we cannot ignore the human rights debate and cannot ignore the fact that much policymaking is now taking place in the language of human rights. In fact, applying a human rights approach to policy debates on development issues is actually a good example of how to *contextualise* biblical principles into secular contexts (see chapter 15) because many basic human rights can be supported from Scripture. The 1948 Universal Declaration of Human Rights enshrines entitlements that most Christians would regard as basic human needs, including the right to practice one's own faith (Article 18), the right to freedom of speech (Article 19) and the right to life (Article 3).

We do not have the space to give a full treatment of human rights from a biblical perspective, but a few thoughts are offered below on how Christians can engage with this debate.

First, we have rights because God has made promises to us, and he is faithful. Israel had covenant rights because God made a promise to them when they agreed the covenant (Ex. 23:20–24:8). This was based not on their intrinsic worth, but on God's love and his initiative. We also have a right, if we believe in Jesus, to become children of God (Jn. 1:12). Again, this right is not based on what we have done, but on what God has done in Christ, and on his faithfulness to his promise.

Secondly, we have rights because God has given all of us responsibility for each other (Ex. 22:22, Jas. 1:27). Rights only have any meaning if someone has the responsibility to provide them so receiving our rights has been made dependent on the actions of others. As Christians, God has given us the responsibility for ensuring that other people receive their rights, so the focus of a Christian approach to human rights has to be on our responsibility to provide for others, not on demanding our rights from others (Prov. 30:8–9). Responsibility towards the poor is a simple example. John makes it very clear that seeing a fellow Christian in physical need creates a responsibility in a brother/sister who has plenty (1 Jn. 3:17). This responsibility to provide for their needs is not a legal obligation but a responsibility of love that heightens rather than diminishes the right of the needy Christian. Here responsibilities and rights are clearly two sides of the same coin.[2]

From the above two points we should be comfortable with the idea that everyone has rights, and comfortable with using the language of rights. Using a *contextualisation* strategy will therefore involve adopting the language of human rights when we agree with the principles involved (e.g. the right to life, the right to education). It becomes a way of securing policy change in the secular arena, using the common language of the day. Human rights also provide a clear legal framework that seeks to avoid the worst forms of abuse and ensure that people have a basic standard of living and can live, as far as possible, in peace and dignity. When lobbying for change, this legal framework is very useful and is a good way to get governments to take their responsibilities for the provision of people's rights more seriously. In fact, it is a good way of getting the government to fulfil their mandate under God. A human rights approach goes beyond a needs based approach (which distributes resources according to the opportunity for greatest impact). It enables every single person to receive what they have been promised under the country's laws and will include the most marginalised groups, who may have previously been excluded.

The crucial question, therefore, is not whether or not rights language is legitimate but whether the right that is being demanded is legitimate. As Christians we would agree with the majority of rights enshrined in international and national laws, but would not agree with some demands for human rights, such as the right to choose when it sanctions abortion on demand.

Another approach in dealing with rights is to emphasise the collective nature of rights, rather than the current emphasis on the individual. This involves emphasising the rights of communities as a way of ensuring poor and oppressed people receive justice. For instance, people who have been unjustly removed from their land can lobby on the basis of a right to security or a right to land. Indigenous communities who are denied access to education or healthcare can lobby the government on behalf of the whole community, arguing that their rights are the same as those of everyone else in the country.

Finally, Christians are sometimes called to give up their rights for the sake of obedience to God or furtherance of the gospel (as the apostle Paul did; see 1 Cor. 9). As Christians we are sometimes called to suffer and we can choose to accept that as an act of obedience. This does not mean we no longer have rights, just that we choose not to exercise them. We may elect to give up these rights (e.g. to security, to community and even to life), if we choose to obey his calling above all else (e.g. to become a missionary to a people group that has not heard the gospel; to stand up for justice in a country where repression and torture is common; to preach the gospel where this is against the law). This is not suffering for suffering's sake, or self-denial for self-denial's sake, but is sacrifice in obedience to a particular calling of God.

Questions for Reflection

- In what circumstances would you consider engaging in acts of civil disobedience?
- What dangers are there in civil disobedience and how would you avoid these?
- Do you think a Christian should use a human rights approach to policymaking? If so, how and when?
- When might you give up your rights?

Further Reading

Carson, Clayborne (ed.), *The Autobiography or Martin Luther King Jr.*

Maggay, Melba Padilla, *Transforming Society*

Wink, Walter, *Engaging the Powers: Discernment and Resistance in a World of Domination*

Conclusion

It is clear from the Bible that God is concerned about injustice. His character, commands and actions all testify to this. When Jesus announces his mission, he says:

> The Spirit of the LORD is on me, because he has anointed me to preach good news to the poor. He has sent me to proclaim freedom for the prisoners and recovery of sight for the blind, to release the oppressed, to proclaim the year of the LORD's favour … and he began by saying to them 'today this Scripture is fulfilled in your hearing' (Lk. 4:18–19, 21).

The 'year of the LORD's favour' refers back to the Year of the Jubilee in Leviticus 25. The purpose of the Jubilee law was to restore things to how they were when Israel first entered the Promised Land when everyone had enough land, everyone was free, people lived in their clans and families, and the land was fertile. Jesus is therefore saying that his kingdom is a kingdom of the Jubilee principle; justice is a central part.

By adding 'today this is fulfilled in your hearing' he was showing that this kingdom is a current reality. It is not something that just exists in the future, even though it will not come fully until Christ returns. It is good news for the poor: good news to those who are on the margins of society, who are excluded in some way, who are denied basic needs and rights or who suffer injustice. This is because when Christians live lives based on the principles of the kingdom (e.g. through sharing their food and belongings with the poor, seeking justice, defending the rights of the oppressed and helping those in need), the poor will experience something of God's blessing.

Furthermore, God is working to redeem the world in which we live. It is destined for renewal and not for destruction. It is a privilege to be used by God to work with him to bring about his kingdom in all its fullness. This means getting involved in evangelism and prayer, worship and discipleship. It also means caring for those in need, speaking out against idolatry and injustice, holding those in power to account for their actions and becoming involved in political activity. Not everyone will be involved in all of these activities, but it is vital that the church as a whole is faithful to the whole of its calling.

A history of Christian involvement shows that when even a few individuals get involved then significant change is possible. Christians, such as Wilberforce, Wesley and Martin Luther King Jr, have been at the forefront of many social movements and leave us a challenging example to follow. Throughout the world Christians continue to stand up for what they believe is right and to bring people a complete gospel of the good news of Jesus Christ. Reconciliation in Rwanda, freeing prisoners in Peru and protecting children in the UK from solvent abuse are just a few examples.

The evangelical church is starting to reclaim its rightful place at the centre of the local community and of society at large. The challenge to each of us is to think about where we see our role in bringing about God's kingdom, how we think God will use us to bring good news to the poor and to challenge the injustices we see around us.

'Is your God big enough?' was the question posed at the end of the introduction.

Is your God big enough that he has defeated all the powers on the cross and everything is under his control, or are there some events that he can do nothing about?

Is your God big enough to transform the world, or is he restricted only to saving individuals and leaving the world to decay?

Is your God big enough that he is on the side of the poor and is passionate about injustice, or does he look at the world with a disinterested detachment?

Is your God big enough to give you all that you need for the task to which he has called you, or will he leave you struggling?

Is your God big enough that he can use even your most faltering efforts to bring about his kingdom, or does he only use experts?

Is your God big enough that he cares about obedience in every aspect of the lives of his followers, or are there some things he is happy to overlook because they are too difficult?

Clearly, God is big enough for all of these things, but the question is whether *our* God is big enough. The question is whether we have faith the size of a mustard seed in an all-powerful and all-loving God who intervenes in his world to bring about his kingdom. If so, he promises that he will use his people to bring about his purposes and that he will give us all that we need (Eph. 6:13–18).

There is also the question whether, even if we believe in such a God, we are willing to get involved. Are we willing to make sacrifices in our own lives and suffer unpopularity or discomfort? Are we willing to support fellow Christians and be supported by them? Are we willing to challenge them and be challenged by them?

If so, this challenge and support will enable us to worship God more effectively, to be more obedient to his will and to be transformed more into his likeness. It will enable us to be a more visible sign of his kingdom:

> Therefore I urge you, brothers and sisters, in view of God's mercy, to offer your bodies as living sacrifices, holy and pleasing to God – this is your spiritual act of worship. Do not conform any longer to the pattern of this world, but be transformed by the renewing of your mind. Then you will be able to test and approve what God's will is – his good, pleasing and perfect will (Rom. 12:1–2).

To conclude, I have included below a poem I found by Njonjo Mue, a Kenyan, stuck on a wall in an office in Nairobi. It serves as a challenge to each one of us to stand for kingdom values that challenge the values of the world, and to stand in solidarity with those who are doing the same. What could happen if you, too, got involved?

Will you too shun me?

When I choose to swim upstream
To question everything given me
When I prefer to keep nothing
In order to have all things
When I refuse to fit the mould
That they have created for me
And when they tell you that I'm mad
For not fitting into
Their particular brand
Of sanity
Will you, too, shun me?

When I choose to go to jail
So as to be truly free
When I prefer life in an asylum

To escape the madness outside
When I choose to give up my dreams
So that others can live theirs
And when I give in to pain
So that the healing can begin
Will you take their side?
Will you, too, shun me?

When I stand up to them
And refuse to follow blindly
And when, by so doing,
I challenge even your own values
When I choose alone to start
What all have been too terrified
To imagine
Will you exchange sanity for comfort?
Will you, too, shun me?

Or will you have the presence of mind
To remember our time together
To recall the warmth, the laughter;
Will you pause and reflect
On who I was to you
And who you know me to be;
And will you then pray for courage
To stand with me,
Or will you, too, shun me?

Notes

Preface
[1] For more information see < www.tearfund.org >.
[2] For more information see < www.micahnetwork.org >.

Introduction
[1] Carson, Clayborne (ed.), *The Autobiography of Martin Luther King Jr.*

Chapter 2
[1] Donald B. Kraybill, *The Upside-down Kingdom*.
[2] Ibid.
[3] Melba Padilla Maggay, *Transforming Society*.

Chapter 3
[1] René Padilla, *The Poor* (occasional paper).
[2] Gary A. Haugen, 'Integral Mission and Advocacy', in Tim Chester (ed.), *Justice Mercy and Humility: Integral Mission and the Poor*.
[3] Alfonso Wieland, *In Love With His Justice*.
[4] Taken from Joseph Hanlon, *Dictators and Debt*, and Congo Country Report on < www.jubileeplus.org/databank/profiles/drcongo.htm >.
[5] Sometimes this collection of activities is called political involvement. Other times it is referred to as advocacy. Throughout the book we will mainly refer to it under the broad banner of working for social justice.

[6] Gary A. Haugen, *Good News About Injustice: A Witness of Courage in a Hurting World*.

[7] Ibid.

[8] I am indebted to Dewi Hughes for this. He retold it to me from memory. It is understood that the parable may not be original to Gitari.

[9] Much of this section is based on Paul Woolley, *A Christian View of Government*.

[10] Maggay, *Transforming Society*.

[11] Ibid.

Chapter 4

[1] Maggay, *Transforming Society*.

[2] Ibid.

[3] Ibid.

[4] R. Paul Stevens, *Abolition of the Laity: Vocation, Work and Ministry in a Biblical Perspective*.

[5] Adapted from Stevens, *Abolition*.

[6] Wallace and Mary Brown, *Angels of the Walls*.

[7] Ibid.

[8] Quoted in *The Observer* (16 February 2003).

[9] < www.henryolonga.com >.

[10] Taken from Gary A. Haugen, 'Integral Mission and Advocacy', in Chester, (ed.), *Justice, Mercy and Humility*. Many more examples appear in Haugen, *Good News*.

[11] Carson (ed.), *Martin Luther King*.

Chapter 5

[1] See Stevens, *Abolition*, for a more detailed consideration of the roles of prophet, priest and king.

[2] Ibid.

[3] Maggay, *Transforming Society*.

Chapter 6

[1] A good place to start for a fuller overview is Lion Handbook, *The History of Christianity*.

[2] Ernest L. Fortin, in the introduction to Augustine, *Political Writings*.

[3] Ibid.

[4] Augustine, *The City of God*, IV.17.

[5] Taken from Anthony C. Thiselton, 'An Age of Anxiety', in Lion Handbook, *History Of Christianity*.

[6] A good summary can be found in John Stott, *Issues Facing Christians Today*. Details of the history of evangelical re-engagement can also be found in René Padilla, 'Integral Mission and its Historical Development', in Chester, (ed.), *Justice, Mercy and Humility*, pp. 42–58.

[7] Taken from James Dunn, 'Pentecostalism and the Charismatic Movement', in Lion Handbook, *History Of Christianity*.

[8] Wesley A. Roberts, 'Martin Luther King', in Lion Handbook, *History Of Christianity*.

[9] Carson (ed.), *Martin Luther King*.

[10] Ibid.

[11] Leonardo Boff and Clodovis Boff, *Introducing Liberation Theology*.

[12] Ibid.

[13] Ibid.

[14] René Padilla, 'Integral Mission and its Historical Development', in Chester (ed.), *Justice, Mercy and Humility*.

[15] Ibid.

[16] See John Stott, *Making Christ Known: Historic Mission Documents from the Lausanne Movement, 1974–1989*; quoted in René Padilla, 'Integral Mission and its Historical Development', in Chester (ed.), *Justice, Mercy and Humility*.

Chapter 7

[1] Based on interviews in Kigali, Rwanda, January 2003.

[2] Philip Yancey, *What's So Amazing About Grace?*

[3] < www.rwanda1.com/government/justice.htm >

[4] In January 2003, 40,000 suspects were released on bail because they were either in category 2 and had confessed or in categories 3 or 4, meaning that their time in prison was already beyond the assigned length of their sentence.

[5] Press release, 'Africa Rights', 23 January 2003.

Chapter 8

[1] Based on Interviews in Quezon City, The Philippines, February 2003.

[2] Policy Paper on Prostitution (Samaritana, 2002).

[3] Ibid.

[4] Details on how to do this are provided in Haugen, *Good News*.

Chapter 9

[1] *Movimiento Revolucionario de Tupac Amaru.*

[2] Based on the account in Wieland, *In Love With His Justice*.

[3] This case is covered in Ruiz, Wullie, 'Celdas que Alababan al Señor', in *Probados por Fuego: testimonios de coraje y esperanza tras las rajas.*

[4] Wieland, *In Love With His Justice*.

[5] Quoted in *Global Action Network 3* (Tearfund, 1998).

[6] Ruiz, 'Celdas que Alababan al Señor'.

[7] Wieland, *In Love With His Justice*.

[8] Ibid.

Chapter 10

[1] Based on interviews in Nairobi, Kenya, January 2002.

Chapter 11

[1] Based on interviews in Kampot Province, Cambodia, March 2003.

Chapter 12

[1] *Global Development Finance* (World Bank, 2002), quoted on < www.jubileedebtcampaign.org.uk/default.asp?action=article &ID=216 >.

[2] Nick Buxton, 'Debt Cancellation and Civil Society', in Paul Gready (ed.), *Fighting for Human Rights*.

[3] R. Greenhill, A. Pettifor, H. Northover and A. Sinha, *Did the G8 Drop the Debt? 5 Years after the Birmingham Human Chain, what has been achieved, and what more needs to be done?*

[4] Marlene Barrett (ed.), *The World Will Never be the Same Again.*

⁵ Quoted in Barrett (ed.), *The World Will Never be the Same Again*.

⁶ < www.hm-treasury.gov.uk/newsroom_and_speeches/ >.

⁷ Barrett (ed.), *The World Will Never be the Same Again*.

⁸ Greenhill et al., *Did the G8 Drop the Debt?*

⁹ BBC Radio 4 `Any Questions', 26 September 1998.

¹⁰ Quoted in Buxton, 'Debt Cancellation and Civil Society'.

Chapter 13

¹ Quoted in Barrett (ed.), *The World Will Never be the Same Again*.

² Taken from an Amnesty International Urgent Action leaflet.

Chapter 14

¹ Graham Gordon, *Advocacy Toolkit 1 & 2*.

Chapter 15

¹ March for Jobs and Freedom, Washington, 28 August 1963.

² Wieland, *In Love With His Justice*.

³ Carson (ed.), *Martin Luther King*.

⁴ See section on further reading at the end of the chapter.

⁵ The unity and continuity of Scripture is a greater reality than the historical discontinuities and changing cultural contexts. In fact, the variety of historical situations that shape the moral teaching of the Bible makes it easier to identify underlying principles and how they might be applied in different contexts. According to Richard B. Hays there are four ways in which the Bible provides this moral guidance: (1) Direct *rule or command*, such as the prohibition of divorce or the commandment not to steal or murder. (2) *Principles*, such as the command to love our neighbour. The meaning of this principle will only become apparent from a general study of the Bible and particularly from an understanding of God's final revelation in the person of Jesus Christ. Once we have grasped something of its meaning it can be applied to a whole variety of different circumstances. (3) The *paradigm* where characters model exemplary behaviour, such as the parable of the Good Samaritan (Lk. 10:25–37). In this

case the paradigm was presented by Jesus to illustrate the meaning of the principle of loving your neighbour. (4) The *symbolic world* of the New Testament, which is the Bible's perspective on the *context* in which all human action and moral decision takes place. This includes God's relationship to creation and the description of human nature and the human condition in general as a result of the rejection of God's authority. A good example is Paul's description of the human condition in Romans 1:18–32. It is important to be aware of which way the Bible is providing guidance in order to know how to interpret a specific passage. See Richard B. Hays, *The Moral Vision of the New Testament: A Contemporary Introduction to New Testament Ethics.*

Chapter 16

[1] Walter Wink, *Engaging the Powers: Discernment and Resistance in a World of Domination*; Kraybill, *Upside-down Kingdom.*

[2] Based on a section in Dewi Hughes, *Castrating Culture: A Christian Perspective on Ethnic Identity from the Margins.*

Bibliography

Anvil Trust, *Workshop Course Notes on The Kingdom of God, The Church and the State, Crime and Justice and The Vision (Shalom)* (Sheffield: Anvil Trust, 2000/01)

Augustine, *Political Writings* (Indianapolis: Hackett, 1994)

Barrett, Marlene (ed.), *The World Will Never be the Same Again* (London: Jubilee 2000, 2002)

Bauckham, R., *The Bible in Politics: How to Read the Bible Politically* (London: SPCK, 1989)

Boff, Leonardo and Clodovis Boff, *Introducing Liberation Theology* (London: Burns & Oates, 1987)

Bosch, David, *Transforming Mission* (New York: Orbis, 1992)

Brown, Wallace and Mary, *Angels of the Walls* (Eastbourne: Kingsway, 2000)

Carson, Clayborne (ed.), *The Autobiography of Martin Luther King Jr.* (London: Abacus, 2002)

Catherwood, Fred, *It Can be Done: The Real Heroes of the Inner City* (Cambridge: Lutterworth, 2000)

Chester, Tim, *Awakening to a World of Need: The Recovery of Evangelical Social Concern* (Leicester: IVP, 1993)

—— (ed.), *Justice, Mercy and Humility: Integral Mission and the Poor* (Carlisle: Paternoster, 2002)

Cook, David, *The Moral Maze: A Way of Exploring Christian Ethics* (London: SPCK, 1999)

Ellul, Jacques, *The Presence of the Kingdom* (2nd edn; Colorado Springs: Helmers & Howard, 1989)

Freire, Paulo, *Pedagogy of the Oppressed* (2nd edn; London: Penguin 1996)

Goldsworthy, Graeme, *Gospel and Kingdom* (Carlisle: Paternoster, 1994)

Gordon, Graham, *Advocacy Toolkit 1 & 2* (Teddington: Tearfund, 2002)

Gourevitch, Philip, *We Wish to Inform you that Tomorrow we will be Killed with our Families* (London: Picador, 1999)

Gready, Paul (ed.), *Fighting for Human Rights* (forthcoming)

Greenhill, R., A. Pettifor, H. Northover and A. Sinha, *Did the G8 Drop the Debt? 5 Years after the Birmingham Human Chain, what has been achieved, and what more needs to be done?* (London: Jubilee Research/CAFOD/Jubilee Debt Campaign, 2003)

Hanlon, Joseph, *Dictators and Debt* (London: Jubilee 2000, 1998)

Haugen, Gary, *Good News About Injustice: A Witness of Courage in a Hurting World* (Downers Grove/Leicester: InterVarsity Press/Inter-Varsity Press, 1999)

Hays, Richard B., *The Moral Vision of the New Testament: A Contemporary Introduction to New Testament Ethics* (Edinburgh: T. & T. Clark, 1997)

Hughes, Dewi, *Castrating Culture: A Christian Perspective on Ethnic Identity from the Margins* (Carlisle: Paternoster, 2002)

——, and Matthew Bennett, *God of the Poor* (Carlisle: OM, 1998)

Kraybill, Donald B., *The Upside-down Kingdom* (2nd edn; Scottdale: Herald, 1990)

Lattimer, Mark, *The Campaigning Handbook* (London: The Directory of Social Change, 2000)

Lion Handbook, *The History of Christianity* (2ⁿᵈ edn; Oxford: Lion, 1990)

Maggay, Melba Padilla, *Transforming Society* (Oxford: Regnum, 1994)

Mott, Stephen, *Biblical Ethics and Social Change* (New York/Oxford: Oxford University Press, 1982)

Myers, Bryant L., *Walking with the Poor: Principles and Practices of Transformational Development* (New York: Orbis, 1999)

Paz y Esperanza, *Probados por Fuego: Testimonios de Coraje y Esperanza tras las Rejas* (Lima: Asociación Paz y Esperanza, 1999)

Pollock, John, *George Whitefield and the Great Awakening* (Oxford: Lion, 1972)

Prunier, Gerald, *The Rwandan Crisis: History of a Genocide* (London: Hurst, 1995)

Schluter, Michael (ed.), *Christianity in a Changing World: Biblical Insight on Contemporary Issues* (London: Marshall Pickering, 2000)

Sider, Ron, *Rich Christians in a Age of Hunger* (4ᵗʰ edn; London, Hodder & Stoughton, 1997)

Sine, Tom, *Mustard Seed Versus McWorld: Reinventing Christian Life and Mission for a New Millennium* (London: Monarch, 1999)

Stevens, R. Paul, *The Abolition of the Laity: Vocation, Work and Ministry in a Biblical Perspective* (Carlisle: Paternoster, 1999)

Stott, John, *Making Christ Known: Historic Mission Documents from the Lausanne Movement, 1974–1989* (Carlisle: Paternoster, 1996)

——, *New Issues Facing Christians Today* (3ʳᵈ edn; London: Marshall Pickering 1999)

Swartley, Willard M, *Slavery, Sabbath, War and Women: Case Issues in Biblical Interpretation* (Scottdale: Herald, 1983)

Tearfund, *Advocacy Toolkit* (Teddington: Tearfund, 2002)

Townsend, C and J. Ashcroft, *Political Christians in a Plural Society* (Cambridge: Jubilee Policy Group, 1994)

Wallis, Jim, *The Soul of Politics: A Practical and Prophetic Vision for Change* (London: Fount, 1994)

Wieland, Alfonso, *In Love With His Justice* (Lima: Asociación Paz y Esperanza, 2003)

Wink, Walter, *Engaging the Powers: Discernment and Resistance in a World of Domination* (Minneapolis: Augsburg Fortress, 1992)

Woolley, Paul, *A Christian View of Government* (London: Conservative Christian Fellowship, 2002)

Wright, Chris J.H., *Living as the People of God: The Relevance of Old Testament Ethics* (Leicester: IVP, 1983)

——, *Knowing Jesus Through the Old Testament* (London: Marshall Pickering, 1992)

——, *Walking in the Ways of the Lord: The Ethical Authority of the Old Testament* (Leicester: Apollos, 1995)

Yancey, Philip, *What's so Amazing About Grace?* (Grand Rapids: Zondervan, 1997)

Yoder, John Howard, *The Politics of Jesus* (2nd edn; Grand Rapids/Carlisle: Eerdmans/Paternoster, 1994)

Scripture Index

Index of Individuals and Organisations

General Index